Wednesdays with Bob

Bob Hawke   Derek Rielly

MACMILLAN
Pan Macmillan Australia

First published 2017 in Macmillan by Pan Macmillan Australia Pty Ltd
1 Market Street, Sydney, New South Wales, Australia, 2000

Cataloguing-in-Publication entry is available
from the National Library of Australia
http://catalogue.nla.gov.au

Typeset in 10/14 pt Chronicle Text by Post Pre-press Group, Brisbane
Internal design: Daniel New
Photography: Richard Freeman
Chapter opener images: Shutterstock
Printed by McPherson's Printing Group

The author and the publisher have made every effort to contact copyright holders for
material used in this book. Any person or organisation that may have been overlooked
should contact the publisher.

For Jones, Gard and Shawnee
and the miracle of second heartbeats.

D. R.

CONTENTS

'They say that beer destroys your brain. Bobby disproves that 'cause he's still got his marbles. He should be a raving lunatic.'
Col Cunningham, Hawke's friend of forty-five years,
March 2017.

'In the end, nobody has popularity that lasts forever. It's one of the great ironies of politics.'
John Howard, foe turned friend,
January 2017.

CHAPTER 1

THE OLD MAN'S LAMENT

J ULY 2016: BOB HAWKE IS MIDWAY THROUGH A HARANGUE on Machiavelli's assertion that it's better to be feared than loved ('It's bullshit!' he growls), when he stands, theatrically hoicks his jeans upwards, eyeballs me and says, 'Mate, I just gotta have a leak . . .'

What strange interpersonal dynamics we have already. After only four interviews spread over four Wednesday afternoons, the country's greatest living politician feels compelled to let the interviewer know he needs to use the toilet instead of excusing himself and briefly disappearing.

But this isn't any ordinary politician. This isn't any ordinary Australian.

'He always looked to Australians like the quintessential Aussie bloke and talked like the quintessential Aussie bloke,' Hawke's loyal pal Kim Beazley had told me.

How quintessentially Australian?

When John F. Kennedy was shot dead in 1963, Hawke was campaigning in the Victorian electorate of Corio, his first attempt to win a seat in the federal parliament.

His campaign manager came to him, breathless. 'Kennedy is dead!' he said.

Hawke's face went white. *'Graham Kennedy is . . . dead?'*

Hawke was the man who blew away the fog of prime ministerial power with a connection to the Australian people that was never severed over four elections. If Menzies was the suffocating conservative, Whitlam imperial and Fraser shorn from the aristocratic grazing class to become a divisive brute, Hawke was the beer-inhaling rogue who also happened to be a Rhodes Scholar.

The word 'messianic' gets thrown around generously when talk turns to Bob Hawke. But the trajectory of little Bobby Hawke is, literally, biblical.

When he was three he was serving as Jesus' envoy to the invalids of Bordertown, South Australia, administering his father's sermons when the Congregational minister was indisposed.

His mother Ellie made her eight-year-old son sign a pledge that he would never drink and predicted Bobby's ascent to the prime ministership before he was born, when her Bible kept falling open to Isaiah 9:6. The passage reads: 'For unto us a child is born, unto us a son is given, and the government shall be upon his shoulders . . . And he will be called Wonderful Counselor, Mighty God, Everlasting Father, Prince of Peace.'

As Hawke's first attorney-general and later foreign minister, Gareth Evans recalls the mood of 1983, when Hawke assumed the ALP leadership: 'We were in the presence of someone who a lot of people perceived as God.'

And here he is on a July afternoon in Sydney, a weak sun lighting up the channels and fjords of a face that has occupied Australian TV screens since the sixties, dying for a piss.

'Now,' says Hawke, 'I do something very unusual.'

He looks at me. Grins.

'I'll have a leak off my balcony.'

Hawke zombie-walks to the southern corner of a terrace,

next to the man-sized sculpture of a bateleur eagle, the cha-pungu, Zimbabwe's national emblem. (Hawke loves the country, hates the dictator. 'Mugabe was one of the most awful men I've ever met,' he says. 'He treated both blacks and whites like shit. He was a very, very unpleasant man. An awful man. It's hard to describe how bad he was.') The difficult soft-shoe shuffle in Skechers memory foam loafers – he'll wear Swiss designer label Bally if he's hitting the town – is a result of peripheral neuropathy, a disorder where malfunctioning nerves jumble the signal between brain, spine and, in Hawke's case, feet. In public Hawke walks either with a cane – a gift from his driver Rob – or supported by his wife of twenty-one years (and lover for over forty) Blanche d'Alpuget. The perception of fragility is deceptive. Hawke's mind is sharp and, though his body is a little stooped, he's still as lean as a greyhound. Inconvenienced, but not at death's door.

I wrestle briefly with the ethics of watching an eighty-six-year-old man unholster. While watching would signal a perversion and an unholy breach of privacy to some, others might expect the journalist to examine every inch of the moment, however intrusive.

I take a middle road.

A swing of the head to capture a split-second of Bob Hawke crisply rocking back on his heels, a clear parabola disappearing into a little drain hole on the terrace's ledge.

He zips, swings around and shuffles back to our interview.
'Better?'
'Yeah. Have I told you about the old man's lament,' says Hawke. He sways from side to side and sings, '*Jiggle, jiggle, dance and dance, the last drop is always in your pants!*'

Laughing, Hawke sits, reassures me that he hasn't got the old man's lament, picks up the cigar and swipes a match.

Am I familiar with Winston Churchill's famous put-downs?

'So many marvellous cracks,' says Hawke. 'Lady Astor and he were at a party and she said to Winston...'

Hawke turns mimic. *'Winston, you're drunk!*

'And you, madam, are ugly, but I will be sober in the morning.

'Another time,' Hawke says, chortling, 'he was in the toilet having a shit when his private secretary knocked on the door and said this public servant had arrived and wanted to see him. Churchill replied, *Tell him one shit at a time is enough!'*

Adman, entrepreneur and horse-owner John Singleton famously switched sides to run the ALP's advertising in the 1987 election at Hawke's behest. The friendship bloomed. Singo's seventieth birthday gift to Hawke of a quarter-share in a promising mare in 1999 netted him over half a million dollars.

Hawke, says Singo, 'is a massively intellectual knockabout. It's a weird combination. He can go on the world stage and discuss any subject at a top level with the president of the United States or the leaders of Russia, China, and change the whole face of Australia, and at the same time be able to drink twenty, thirty beers with you – this is before he went off the beer – love cricket and football and racing and betting, and sit in the cabinet meetings with a form guide on his lap. It's as though they've got him mixed up when they were making him. They didn't know whether to put him in the public bar or the Lodge. So they made him a bit of both.'

— CHAPTER 2 —

THE PITCH

THE IDEA OF WRITING SEVENTY THOUSAND WORDS ON Bob Hawke in his eighty-seventh year had started as a throwaway line at a publisher meet-and-greet three months earlier.

Over cocktails, I tried to sell a surfing memoir that would be part Tim Winton's *Breath*, part *Barbarian Days*, the autobiography by the *New Yorker*'s William Finnegan that had just won a Pulitzer Prize.

The agent gagged theatrically then suggested I might like to try something she could sell instead. Did I have any ideas?

As it happened, I'd always wanted to meet Bob Hawke and I did feel like the passage of time had begun to erase our collective memory of Hawke's career and government.

The pitch: 'I want to secure the legacy of our greatest post-war prime minister.'

The response: 'I know a publisher who loves Bob. Get me a proposal.'

It's as easy as that? Throw out a name, skeleton a chapter outline, and I'm gifted the keys to a man I'd only ever seen on television, whose presence filled my teenage season, culturally and politically?

There's a false start. Turnbull's disastrous double dissolution election has just been called and my idea is to ride in Bob's slipstream during the campaign.

I compile an elaborate description of how I'll follow Bob on the hustings. Bob Hawke and Bill Shorten together. Who's the intellectual superior, the more dazzling of the two close-up? How does the public react to each?

I'll watch Bob campaigning in Tanya Plibersek's seat. Does she swoon in his presence? Does Bob flirt a little?

Bob and I in Perth together, where he delivers a speech at his old high school, Perth Modern, on the importance of a robust economy and a strong social program. A visit to that lonely stretch of road in Kings Park where, seventy years ago, his motorbike slid out from underneath, nearly killing him.

To the television studios on election night, where Bob delivers sage opinion as results tumble in. Later in the year, to the Melbourne Cup, where fans jostle to snatch his image on their phones. To a boozy dinner party with old pals from business, politics, the media and horseracing. To a game of footy where Hawke disappears a beer and the crowd reacts joyously. To a multi-faith event (Bob was famously hot for Israel but regards the misunderstanding of Islam as 'one of the great potential dangers confronting the world') in the name of bringing Jew and Muslim together.

At home with Blanche, the lover turned second wife... Does he read? Write? Garden? Is his charisma as powerful away from the spotlight? Or is he a crotchety old prick jeering and stabbing fingers at the television when there's no one to play up to?

I hear nothing. The proposal withers on the vine.

The next thing I hear is that Bob is frail. So I wind back my expectations. Who needs vaudeville if you can sit at the feet of

Bob Hawke, almost nine years a prime minister, inhaling his cigar vapour and accumulated wisdom? Even in his harvest years, surely the wit and memory is still strong.

I rename the proposal *Wednesdays with Bob*, a take on Mitch Albom's bestselling book *Tuesdays with Morrie*, in which Albom visits his dying college professor one day a week and they talk about happiness, regrets and facing death.

Not that Bob is dying, or close to it. (I'll later discover Hawke greyhound-fit post-workout in a Nike jacket and skinny grey sweatpants.) And not that I've read *Tuesdays with Morrie*, if we're going to be honest. I do know it sold like hell.

A weekend lunch with Blanche is organised. If Blanche likes me, I'll get a chance to front Hawke directly with the idea.

Desperate to be adored, I read a third of Blanche's oeuvre in less than two weeks. I knew she could write, but she can . . . *write*. Her 1982 biography *Robert J. Hawke* is the masterwork that convinced the ALP Hawke had the heft to lead the party.

On Longing draws the reader into her clandestine affair with Hawke through the seventies, its dissolution in 1979 and its revival in 1988, leading to their marriage in 1995.

The more recent historical quartet, beginning with *The Young Lion*, is bawdy as hell. Who knew Louis VII needed milking maids to ensure an even temper?

> **His Majesty's Masturbators, as Eleanor called them, were another cause for argument between Louis and his wife. Louis had assured her, 'I find no pleasure in what they do.'**
>
> **'How strange, sire, the physician does not prescribe similarly unpleasant physic to keep me strong and healthy,' she replied.**

The agent grins. 'She writes sex very well.'

At exactly noon on a midwinter Sunday, Blanche d'Alpuget sweeps into the vaulted-ceiling elegance of Sydney's Bistro Moncur, looking absolutely nothing like her richly lived seventy-two years. My powers of observation are neutralised by her long lashes, tornado of fine gold hair and, as a new convert to her writing, intellectual authority.

I've learned Blanche is a Francophile (emails to the agent commence with *Ma très chère* and close with *Bisous*) and so I call her Madame d'Alpuget (unaware there's an emphasis on the 'u') and trip over my feet as I lunge to kiss her on each cheek while she offers a hand.

'We can shake later,' she says, surprised.

My proposal slides into the conversation that has bounced back and forth between Blanche and the agent around the forty-five-minute mark, once the gossip surrounding political and literary figures is cleared away.

'So tell me about your idea for Bob . . .' Blanche looks at me expectantly.

My prepared speech is a little stilted, which is always a problem when you don't have the game to fire off the cuff, but it doesn't seem to offend.

'I want to, uh, create an essential document that snatches Bob in the second half of his eighty-seventh year. If *Robert J. Hawke: A Biography* convinced the ALP that Bob was ready for the leadership, *Bob Hawke at Eighty-Six* will remind Australia why we fell for him so hard.'

'You'll have to get it past his office manager!' Blanche hoots, her verbal approximation of an exclamation mark. 'But send me the outline and I'll put it in front of her.'

Later.

Dear Blanche,

Did I embarrass myself with the fawning Young Lion *questions? It's always a little surreal to be deep in a novel and to meet its creator. And, in this case, I'd just re-read* Robert J. Hawke *and* On Longing, *so the spell was stronger than usual.*

Anyway, more than anything, I believe we need to firmly lasso Bob's legacy.

Book proposal attached.

Yours . . .

Twenty-four hours pass without a reply. I figure I'm out. I experience professional failure regularly enough to be okay with rejection, but, goddamn it, so close!

Then . . .

Ding!

Dear Derek,

You're in luck. Bob laughed at the 'sitting in a cloud of cigar smoke' and said yes. He feels no need to run it past the office wife.

Hawke will later tell me, 'Jill Saunders has been with me since 1983, from the day of my election as party leader and has been an indispensable part of my success.'

I'll ask her for an update of his calendar and get back to you with free days. Always afternoons, as he likes to sleep late and do crossword puzzles. You may want to do more than one a week. I didn't mention that to him, but if you do it's something you and he can discuss.

Best wishes,

Blanche

PS There is another book with a lot of info about Bob, but it's hard to get hold of. It's Mediator: A Biography of Sir Richard Kirby, *by moi, published by MUP in the 1970s. I have only one copy and won't lend it, even to good and trustworthy people like you. It's not essential reading because you're writing about him now, but it shows what a young firebrand he was when he was advocate for the ACTU and nearly gave the judges who listened to his arguments apoplexy because he was so disrespectful to Their Honours. And so abrasive. It covers ten years of his life. He became a rock star then, in 1958.*

Nine days later, I was parked out the front of chez Hawke–d'Alpuget, formerly chez Hawke–Hawke, rehearsing banter and wondering if the whole idea was infantile self-deception. Me? Unlimited access to this man?

But there I was. Standing at the gate of Bob Hawke's house with a bagful of recording devices and three sheets of questions. Deep breath. Buzzer hit.

— CHAPTER 3 —

THE PRIME MINISTER GREETS HIS GUEST

I NSIDE. A CITRUS SUN SOAKS THE WATERFRONT HOUSE BUILT on 952 square metres of elevated bushland on Sydney's lower north shore; the prized piece of dirt in a blue-ribbon Liberal seat bought, unseen, at auction during the recession of 1991 for $1.23 million. The old timber house was knocked down and a four-level home with rooftop putting green was built.

A 500-kilogram sculpture from Zimbabwe of an African woman's head, with headdress, greets visitors in the foyer. Through an open door, a chair – bought in a Botswana market and whose postage to Australia cost considerably more than the chair itself – is fashioned to appear as a woman with a water jar on her head, inviting you to sit in her lap.

This is Blanche's home office, where emails are read and answered, appointments sought and made. If you were to step into this room, you'd see across a stair void and through a large window, and into Hawke's own, largely ornamental, study. Blanche's serious writing space is an ugly little flat in Cammeray, a six-minute drive away, where the computer has no access to email, where no phone calls are allowed and where, most importantly, there is no view to distract the writer. Blanche stops work once an hour to blink and stretch.

At the entrance to the north-facing terrace on the second floor is the sculpture *Whatever*, which depicts a longitudinally distorted man wearing a hooded jumper and with his hands in his pockets, the insouciance obvious. It was made using a 3D printer by Blanche's son Louis Pratt, who arrived for a three-week stay in 2009 and has lived in the house's boatshed ever since.

And it's here, on the threshold of the terrace, overlooking the yachts of Sailors Bay, where Mr Bob Hawke, who is eighty-six years old, has left his sudokus and cryptic crossword to examine the visitor.

The eagle face and roaring hair are so familiar, the visitor feels like he's addressing an old friend. The rehearsed greetings ('Oh, Mr Hawke, it's a pleasure beyond my imagination to be in your company ...' 'Good afternoon, Mr Hawke, I'm extremely delighted to ...') are forgotten.

'Mate. Mate. *Hello ... mate!*'

'Did you bring a cigar?' Hawke greets me in return.

I present a $45 Davidoff from the Dominican Republic, Hawke gently repeating the name to correct me on the pronunciation. (Note: lengthen the 'a' – *Daaahvidoff*.) The shopkeeper had placed the cigar in a plastic bag with a photograph of a cancerous mouth, although I have disposed of the state-mandated packaging prior to presentation.

I tell Hawke I hope these interviews will lasso his legacy and, by virtue of what I presume is still the sparkling intellect I witnessed growing up, demonstrate the drudgery of modern politics.

What I don't reveal is my fear that Australia's most-loved prime minister, whose 75 per cent approval rating in 1984 is better than the combined total of the current prime minister and his opposite, has been out of the game for so long there is a danger his charisma, the breadth of his achievements, the scope of his wisdom, will be forgotten.

Is this a fan book? Maybe it is.

Or maybe it's the natural result of nostalgia for a time when politics did mean something to a young man; when the great game had the potential to engage not alienate; when the media didn't manipulate every honestly spoken word, thereby creating a climate in which a politician, if he values his existence, must robotically repeat, and never deviate from, carefully vetted slogans. A time when politicians, or at least this one, arrived on a platform of ideas, with an inquisitive, intellectual nature, and therefore wasn't harnessed to immovable positions.

Three days before his election as prime minister in 1983, Hawke had fronted the National Press Club in Canberra, dazzling, cajoling and teasing the mob like no one before or since.

I watched the footage on the news as a teenage boy, hypnotised by the revelation that a stud was going to wrench the tiller away from that overweening broomstick, Malcolm Fraser. From the post of my older brother's bed swung a necklace with a plastic disc that read: *Shame Fraser, shame.*

Hawke's reply to a question about the press going soft on him during the campaign: 'I've been around in public life since the early sixties. If it's a honeymoon, it's about time we consummated it.'

And there was his exchange with a reporter who accused the prime ministerial candidate of secretly betting on the election. For any other politician, the question was potentially ruinous. It demanded a careful answer. Circumspection. An avoidance of admission. For Hawke, it was an opportunity to further cement – as if the further application of cement was necessary – his everyman appeal.

Reporter: 'Would you care to comment on a weekend newspaper report that had a sixty-thousand-dollar betting plunge made on your beha—by people . . .'

Hawke (jauntily): 'You went very close to being. . . you were dangerously close there – you were going to say on my behalf, weren't you?'

The crowd roared.

Reporter: 'If I could go on . . . reportedly, within the ALP, and can I quote from the report, sixty thousand dollars is believed to be part of a nationwide betting plunge organised by sources close to ALP leader Mr Hawke. Nationwide plunge on Labor is masterminded by a known Canberra figure.'

Hawke (through the crowd's laughter): 'Well, I don't know what people around me are doing. I must say that they've been very close to me most of the time . . . [pulls earlobe] . . . but they have snuck off to do other things, I understand, occasionally . . . [crowd laughs] . . . It may be that because they think they're not sufficiently well-paid they've tried to add to their income by having a bet . . .'

When was the last time the sight of an Australian politician caused people to weep with joy? The chief political correspondent for the *Sydney Morning Herald* at the time, Paul Kelly, witnessed the phenomenon himself.

'This was very early, February 1983, just after he'd disposed of [former ALP leader] Hayden,' says Kelly. 'The campaigning has started. Fraser's called the election. We went to Brisbane with Hawke and he had a street walk along Queen Street on a Saturday morning. This was his first street walk as the new Labor leader and the crowd reaction was extraordinary. People just flocked to him, particularly women, housewives doing the shopping. Some of them were crying. The sense of emotion and delight and hope was amazing, and I said to a colleague at the time, "I know it's the opening days of the campaign, but as far as I'm concerned you can put down the binoculars."'

Kelly explains the crowd's reaction: 'Fraser had had three terms as prime minister and the third term hadn't been terribly successful. And while Bill Hayden was a highly competent leader of the Labor Party, and Hayden had done very well in the 1980 election, there was a . . . unique . . . quality to Hawke. He was able to really inspire public opinion and harness a lot more popular support as leader. And so the things Hawke campaigned on were reconciliation, recovery and reconstruction, which were quite powerful ideas at the time. Hawke offered hope to a country divided by Fraser.'

Even the prime minister's wife, Tamie Fraser, fell under Hawke's spell, describing him as 'sexy' and adding, 'Like most women in Australia, I quite like him.'

A newspaper headline the following morning was the world's most succinct, and public, cuckolding.

HAWKE. SEXY. TAMIE.

In the book *Time of Testing*, that follows the build-up to the 1983 election, Craig McGregor describes witnessing the hero-worship amongst Hawke's supporters. The crowd clapped and reached out to him, parting 'like the Red Sea' as he approached the stage. They hung on his every word. He looked 'like some mythic figure . . . in a corrupt world, [he was] the image of a plain man, good and true, keeping faith with the people.'

A brief examination of Hawke's eight years and nine months of government reveals the sweeping scope of his achievements: Four election victories. Australia opened to global markets via the floating of the dollar and the deregulation of the financial system. Consensus between employers and unions, saving the economy from the inflationary devil of indexed wage increases. The spigot to universal healthcare turned back on after Fraser binned it, reinventing Medibank as Medicare. Australia, in cahoots with Jacques Cousteau and the French government, saving Antarctica from mining for fifty years. The Gordon River in Tasmania saved from damming by the state government. Compulsory superannuation paid by employers. Unemployed benefits indexed to inflation. Retention rates in high school lifted from 30 to 70 per cent. Little Australia so instrumental in the abolition of apartheid that Nelson Mandela and Bob Hawke would become firm friends, Mandela telling Hawke during a visit to Australia in 1990 that he was here today 'because of you'.

Take off the rose-coloured glasses and the Hawke government also oversaw the worst recession since the Great Depression. Houses and businesses were lost when interest rates on mortgages soared to 17 per cent as the government moved too late to knife an asset bubble. (It's inescapably ironic that Hawke was able to afford the waterfront hunk of land his house sits on because of the plunge in property prices during the recession.)

And the miserable end to Hawke's prime ministership: the electorate delivering a satisfaction rating of 28 per cent as Paul Keating carped from the sidelines, destabilising, contradicting. 'We've never had one leader, not one,' Keating claimed, twisting the dagger further with, 'Leadership is not about being popular. It's about being right and about being strong.'

'Paul's performance was vainglorious and arrogant, disloyal and contemptuous of everyone on the political stage but himself,' the deposed prime minister wrote in *The Hawke Memoirs*. 'Paul, unable to come to terms with or to understand the rapport I enjoyed with the Australian public, made disparaging references to me, glibly reducing my leadership style to "tripping over television cables in shopping centres".'

'Keating was a saboteur, pure and simple,' says Paul Kelly.

Hawke prepares the Davidoff.

He snips the end off with one of the two cutters on the table, takes the cigar in his mouth, and strikes a match. He lets the match burn for a few seconds to get rid of the sulphur smell. He then avoids touching the cigar directly with the flame. To aficionados like Hawke, the lighting of a fresh cigar is an art. The smoker must kiss it gently, drawing the smoke slowly, lest too much air is pushed through the cigar and it overheats, ruining its quality.

'I dunno what we're going to talk about,' says Hawke, sceptical that there's anything of value left to mine after his memoirs and his second wife Blanche's books, including the seminal *Robert J. Hawke* and its sequel, *Hawke: The Prime Minister*, Paul Kelly's masterful *The Hawke Ascendancy* as well as a two-part episode of the ABC TV program *Australian Story*, histories of Labor in government, Gareth Evans' *Inside the Hawke–Keating Government: A Cabinet Diary* and an endless ream of newspaper and magazine stories.

I tell Hawke I want to interview him about the joy of love. Desire. Finding true love through infidelity. Fatherhood. Success. Friendship. Religion in the modern world. Sport. The making of a man and what manhood is. Women. The lingering tang of any political bitterness. Enemies. The state of geopolitics. Death.

And sconcing, of course.

Sconcing is the Oxford University tradition of making students scull two-and-a-half pints (1.4 litres) of ale as punishment for breaches of etiquette (or 'grievous sins') in relation to dinner in the university's great hall. Arrive late, forget your gown or start eating before the saying of grace had concluded and you had to drain the sconce in twenty-five seconds or less.

Hawke's record of eleven seconds, set in 1955, was as pivotal to his enduring popularity, he says, as the statesmanship that would protect a pristine continent for two generations and ensure the long-term prosperity of Australia.

As one university don described Hawke at the time: 'In summer he drank excessively, wenched excessively, played cricket excessively. We thought he was going to the dogs. When winter came, he stopped drinking, stopped wenching, and studied excessively. We thought he'd do himself an injury from overwork. But when summer came he forgot the library, returned to his girls and his beer. That was Digger for you.'

At my first meeting with Hawke – who today is squeezed into an Italian-made black leather bomber jacket that would appear fashionable on a twenty-year-old (a gift from a friend) and raw denim jeans, with a hearing aid peeled over his left ear and neck wrapped in a gold chain – it seems appropriate to investigate, before anything else, this ability to evaporate beer.

'I was born with one of those throats that just opens,' says Hawke. 'The president of the junior common room then had to drink one and beat the time. But he had no chance. He spattered it all over himself.'

It's a trait that remains undiminished by age. Search YouTube and you'll find videos of Hawke in various locations disappearing schooners of beer, even as he approaches ninety.

At the Sydney Cricket Ground in January 2017, Australian batsman Peter Handscomb, who'd just scored a century, was asked what he thought the highlight of the day was: his century or Bob Hawke sculling a beer, which was played live on a giant television screen at the ground.

'It was in between overs and he was cheers-ing the crowd, and [fellow batsman] Hilton [Cartwright] and I were talking to each other, like, *Surely not – is he going to do it? Is he going to do it?* As he did we both started going nuts out in the middle. And the crowd joined in as well. It was . . . cool.'

At the centenary of Oxford's Rhodes House in 2003, alongside fellow Rhodes Scholar Bill Clinton, Hawke was asked if he would take another swing – for old time's sake.

'They went fucking mad,' says Hawke. 'They brought the beer in after a couple of courses. We had Clinton standing up with Hillary, going, "Go, Bob! Go, Bob!" I got it down in twenty seconds.'

Hawke's tone is beautiful when he's engaged. Those heavy lids lift and the pale blue eyes pop. Eyebrows like pampas grass invigorated after monsoonal rain shoot northwards. (In 1983, one economics writer imagined a thousand women orgasming every time they shot up.)

While he talks, I stare at the clear brown skin, the precise shave that has missed only one hair, the crown that is still a cyclone swell of marching silver waves. Even two droplets of sweat clinging to his chin can't ruin the tableau.

Hawke isn't the prolific talker I'd imagined from the one-time ACTU advocate who'd harangue the arbitration commission's judges in opening addresses that could last three days and replies that went on and on and on, until, in the words of Sir John Moore, the presiding judge of the Australian Conciliation and Arbitration Commission, 'He physically couldn't stand, except by hanging on to the lectern . . . we were adjourning at regular intervals because his voice was giving out.'

But ask a question and, if he's into it, he'll answer it precisely. If he isn't, Hawke takes his responses to a certain level and then snaps shut.

When I ask his dream of happiness, he says, 'It's being with Blanche. It's impossible to describe the sublime happiness that I experience in our relationship.'

Does he often think about that chance meeting in Jakarta in 1970?

'It comes to mind occasionally. I was on my way to Geneva because I was on the international executive of the International Labour Organization and a friend of mine, a Rhodes Scholar at Oxford, Rawdon Dalrymple – he went on to become one of our leading diplomats – was then our second in the embassy to Indonesia. And we were sitting on a very warm, sunny morning on the verandah of his home in Jakarta and this vision in white walked around the corner. She wore a white dress and was beautifully tanned.'

Was she the most beautiful thing he'd ever seen?

'Yes.'

Was the attraction reciprocated?

'She didn't appear unhappy.'

Did you say anything to Dalrymple after she'd walked away?

'Of course I spoke to him.'

Do you remember what you said?

(Abruptly): 'No.'

When Hawke's done with a topic, he nods and picks up his cigar.

So you wait a little.

He's polite enough to not draw on his cigar if you've asked a question. Even if it's poised on his lips, he'll put it down, answer, pick it back up.

So you wait a little longer. Give him time to circle the vapour in his mouth. Reflect. Consider. Determine what can and can't be told.

After two hours, we've talked near-death experiences, the losing of his religion, the wellspring of love that was his childhood, Mandela, Curtin, Cousteau, his great pals Bush Senior and George Shultz, the disaster of invading Iraq and Afghanistan, the lack of any progress on the Israel–Palestine question (the great disappointment of Obama's presidency, says Hawke) and the curveball of bringing the Chinese in to mediate, the booze, the importance of kids learning Mandarin and . . .

I see a look that says, *Mate, I'm tapped.*

'You had enough?' I ask.

'Just about, yeah . . .'

As I pack away the three recording devices (my paranoia of technical failure was justified: one didn't work), Hawke looks at me, grins, and says, 'This one is off the record.'

He slings me an insight into a significant figure and a major upcoming event in world politics that in print would seem poisonous, a sabotage with tints of international intrigue, but here it is told with a wink and such a boyish grin that it shows what a natural performer he still is.

With that, Hawke snorts a laugh and, like any good eighty-six-year-old, returns to his cryptic crossword.

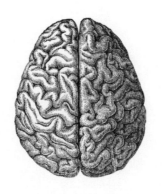

— CHAPTER 4 —

A POP QUIZ

MARCEL PROUST WAS A FOURTEEN-YEAR-OLD IN 1885 when he first filled out a questionnaire for the daughter of the French prime minister, Antoinette Faure. Mademoiselle would invite her friends to answer a series of identical questions designed to reveal the subject's innermost feelings. In 1993 *Vanity Fair* adopted the practice in an abbreviated version, asking notable figures – including Norman Mailer, William F. Buckley Jr, Allen Ginsberg and Salman Rushdie – questions that were then published on the back page. As a warm-up to our dozen interviews, Hawke humours me by participating in something similar. I figure a dozen breezy questions tossed at Hawke will give him a chance to exercise those velvet tonsils.

You good? I ask.

Hawke belts a hit from his cigar then nods, leans forward in his chair, gaze fixed, as alert as if he were a contestant on *Sale of the Century*.

Tell me, what fault do you have the most compassion for?

Hawke swats the question away easily. 'The fault I detest most is a lack of compassion.'

Compassion. The Fatherhood of God and the Brotherhood of Man. They're enduring themes of Hawke at eighty-six, at fifty and at thirteen, when his dad first tutored his son on the inter-connectedness of humanity.

The 2010 telemovie *Hawke* opens with this scene of a post-copulating Bob and Blanche in bed.

Blanche (nude): 'What do you believe in Bob? What *ignites* you?'

Hawke (nude): 'I believe in equality ... honour ... and the Brotherhood of Man.'

All through our interviews Hawke will circle back to the impact his Congregational minister father, Clem, had on him. He'll think for a few seconds then, letting out a long breath, begin his answer: 'It fits in with what I said in the beginning about my father's influence on me ...' Or: 'I can probably best explain it in reference to my father ...'

Hawke says he was 'surrounded by love as a child' and was 'profoundly influenced by the best man I ever knew. I was extraordinarily close to my father and admired him enormously. He said, "Son, if you believe in the Fatherhood of God, you must necessarily believe in the Brotherhood of Man. You are brothers and sisters and you should live that way. You should try your best to improve the lives of others."

'I accepted that and so I've always felt impelled by the reality of that statement, even when I ceased to be a part of organised religion at the end of 1952. I've always felt that we are brothers and sisters and that carries obligations. I would identify that as the major characteristic of my life and the way I've lived my life.'

Arthur Clarence 'Clem' Hawke turned eighty-five the day he saw his son become prime minister in 1983. He greeted reporters that morning by telling the press pack how lucky Australia was to have his son as PM.

Hawke's mother Ellie died in 1979, four years before her son became prime minister. But even now, when Ellie's name is mentioned, the hooded eyelids peel back, the chin lifts and the eyes grow round. For a moment, it isn't Hawke, the eighty-six-year-old with the pacemaker and the hearing aid; it's little Bobby, the precocious three-year-old.

When Clem became a chaplain in the AIF during World War II, the pre-teenage Hawke would stand on the fence at the front of their house in Tate Street, West Leederville, waiting for his father to walk up their street.

Once he'd spotted Clem, Hawke would spring down off his perch and run towards him. 'I just couldn't wait to hug him and have his arms around me,' Hawke recalls. 'When he left I'd give him a big kiss and a hug and tell him he had to come back soon. We had a lovely, natural relationship . . . I just spent most of my time at home. I had a lot of friends but it was such a place of love and happiness. I didn't want to be anywhere else, really. I feel so sorry for kids who don't have a happy home life because it makes a difference to the whole of the rest of your life.'

Is that where you learned the fundamentals of fatherhood? I ask.

Hawke returns to the present, the hoods come down, the years return.

'Well, I didn't learn enough because I was so bloody busy,' says Hawke, who won the 1971 Victorian Father of the Year award while president of the ACTU, despite the fact his first wife, Hazel, was virtually a single parent. 'I just didn't spend enough time with my kids. That's why when I found out that Rosslyn was a heroin addict in 1984 I felt an enormous sense of guilt that I hadn't been a good enough father.'

He continues, 'The first thing is you've got to show your love. And it's got to be a real love. Let your kids know that they matter and that you're going to do everything you can to help them develop their talents. One of the great sorrows in my life, and in hers, is with [eldest daughter] Susan. She was a very good student . . . she was going to do law . . . and then she got this bug about doing work to help prisoners, and she gave up on the law. I said, "Sweetheart, I admire your commitment to helping these people, but that can wait. You've got to equip yourself now because this will determine the rest of your life." She doesn't talk about it to me, but I know she's deeply regretted it. She could have done anything.'

The second of Bob and Hazel's children, Stephen, 'became alienated from me over uranium,' says Hawke. 'That was in 1979 when they had the passionate debate about mining and export of uranium, and Susan and Steve were among those who demonstrated against it. Stephen even changed the surname of his sons. The two grandsons have got their mother's surname. That was deeply hurtful, but I understood. So it's a question of loving your children and encouraging their talents. Steve was a brilliant student. He could've been a multimillionaire, but he devoted his life to the Aborigines. And I'm very proud of him.'

What about faults you see in other people that don't alter your perception of them, that you're happy to indulge?

'If I make a judgement that their heart is in the right place, then I'm happy to try to work with them.'

What do you hate?

'Well, I'm not a hater – and that's an important fact to note. I'm not a hater of people. I can be terribly disappointed and angry with things they say and do, but I'm not a hater. I hate discrimination of any sort based on race, colour or creed. It's just absolute anathema to me. So the institutions, the people who practise it, I hate the effects. And that very much includes sexual discrimination.'

When I ask what historical figures he most despises, Hawke

breathes a bored sigh and runs through the usual list – Adolf, Stalin – before suddenly becoming animated again.

'At a lesser level, although still tragically in terms of the present day, Bush Junior. His decision to invade Iraq was a blunder of massive proportions. And I'm not just being wise after the event. Three weeks before he invaded Iraq, I wrote a piece for *The Australian* newspaper saying that Osama bin Laden must be on his knees morning and night, praying to Allah that Bush will invade, because nothing could do more to boost the cause and the activities of the terrorists.'

Do you believe, Mr Hawke, that Bush Junior's invasion was malicious or did it come from good intentions?

'The fanatics of religion are the problem. And it was the Christian Right in America who pushed him into it. We've got [Tony] Blair. It was his religion that motivated him in the awful decision he made, which has all come out recently [in the Chilcot report]. No, it was not malice. It was prejudice and ignorance.'

Hawke spits out a cloud of smoke in disgust.

'Tony Blair,' says Hawke, 'is an actor. I always feel like saying, "Turn off the acting button." His decision in regard to Iraq was even worse than John Howard's. He just gave carte blanche to George Junior . . . They were both driven by their religion.'

Would you say the effects of the Iraq War have been more disastrous than Vietnam?

'Yes, a much more lasting effect . . . Many of these decisions to automatically go along with them are as bad as the decisions of the Americans themselves. It's interesting that a number of the leading military figures have expressed their view about it, but the politicians involved have never apologised.'

Are there any military events you admire?

'There are just wars, and one which I supported was the first Gulf War. Bush Senior was the president and we were very close and he kept in constant contact with me. Some of my party were against it. They were very short-sighted. You had a situation where a dictator had gratuitously invaded a neighbouring country without a cause, without justification of any kind.

'Then when the war was over, and the Iraqi troops had been driven back across the border, George rang me again. He said, "Bob, I'm being pressured very much by a lot of my people that we should press on to Baghdad and get rid of this monster."

'I said, "No way, George." I said, "You have done a magnificent job in getting together a coalition, with the support of the United Nations and a lot of the Arab states, specifically to eject the Iraqis from Kuwait. It would, in my judgement, be breaking the trust of the people who have joined you to do this."

'He said, "Bob, I can't tell you how glad I am to hear you say that." He said, "That's my view too. We won't be going alone."'

When I ask what historical and contemporary figures he admires, Hawke lists Mandela, whom he assisted from afar with trade union pressure on South Africa's apartheid government in the seventies and as prime minister in the eighties, and Jacques-Yves Cousteau, who helped Hawke to protect Antarctica from mining.

But, more than anyone, Hawke esteems wartime prime minister John Curtin. Hawke's uncle Albert was a significant figure in Western Australian politics, premier for six years and leader of the Labor Party for fifteen, and he once introduced ten-year-old Bobby to Curtin. There are the obvious parallels between Curtin and Hawke, of course. Both drunks. Both being handed the keys to Australia at crucial points in its history: Curtin with Japan on Australia's doorstep in World War II, Hawke with an economy on its knees.

'Even in the dark days of war, he was thinking of Australia *after* the war,' Hawke explains. 'Since the nation was formed at the beginning of the century, Australia had never experienced full employment or anything like it, and he had the idea that the Australia he was fighting to save was going to be a bigger and a better Australia. And so, during the war, he established a Department of Post-War Reconstruction. The head of that was Nugget Coombs, a great Australian public servant.

'They set about planning what Australia was going to be like after the war. And the most significant feature of that, of course, was the commitment to a massive post-war immigration policy, which was the single most important decision ever taken by any Australian government, because it absolutely changed Australia. We opened the country to people from about 180 different nations. While there have been some problems, essentially it's been a peaceful revolution; I'd say the most peaceful change in the composition of any country ever. I hold him in the highest regard for his integrity.'

I switch tack. Of the two parents, I ask, can you recognise what characteristics you inherited from each of them?

'Well, you know what I got from my father . . .'

The Brotherhood of Man.

'From my mother, I got the importance of education, because that was one of my major commitments when I became prime minister: equality of educational opportunity. When I took office, Australia had the lowest retention rate in secondary education of any developed country in the world, only 30 per cent, and I was absolutely dedicated to moving on that immediately, so we brought in means-tested education and educational grants. By the time I was out, it had gone up to 70 per cent.'

What do you believe your main fault is?

'Alcohol has been a problem. Once I made up my mind I was going to pursue a parliamentary career and aim for the prime ministership, I knew I couldn't continue drinking because I couldn't ever do anything to disgrace my country, so I gave it up in May 1980, and I didn't have a drop for thirteen years. I never had a drop while I was prime minister.

'I took it up again in 1993 and, again, on occasions I overdid it. It put a great strain on my relationship with Blanche. She was quite upset at the time. I've gotten on top of it now. I only have a single glass of red every night with dinner.'

(When I ask Blanche later about the one-drink-at-dinner she says that in the early days the glass was more like a bucket.)

How do you want to die?

'On a golf course. Blanche's stepfather did it that way. He completed a round of golf and he was sitting in the cart, filling in the card. Fell over dead. I reckon that was pretty cute.'

Cute!

Hawke's been thinking about death just a little lately, calling the lack of political will to legalise euthanasia 'absurd'.

'It's just an unarguable case. I can see no logical or moral basis for such an absurd position,' he had told ABC Radio National, a week earlier.

Hawke said he and Blanche, who is fourteen years his junior, had an arrangement: 'If I was to lose my marbles . . . then something is done about it. I don't expect it to be a pillow pressed exuberantly over my nose, but I'm sure that she could organise something with a family doctor.'

Not that Hawke sees dementia on the immediate horizon.

'I'm in tremendously good health. And I have an absolute determination that I'm *not* going to lose my marbles. That's why you see me every day doing at least two hard cryptics and a couple of hard sudokus. As you get older, mental exercise is as least as important as physical exercise.'

Is there anything that keeps you awake at night? Night thoughts?

'No. I'm the world's best sleeper. I have at least ten hours a night.'

How did you age so well?

'The most brilliant decision I ever made: my choice of parents.'

Of course, says Hawke, 'The sensible thing to do is to look after your body. Eat well, don't smoke cigarettes.' He pauses and adds, 'Smoke cigars and don't inhale. That's *very* good for you.'

— CHAPTER 5 —

DICK WOOLCOTT

WHAT KIND OF MAN IS HAWKE WHEN THERE ISN'T A microphone conspicuous under his chin? How does he behave among friends, for instance? Does the brotherhood rhetoric match the behaviour of the man who in 1979, while ACTU president, called the leader of the Labor Party, Bill Hayden, 'a lying cunt with a limited future'? (In his defence, he was extremely well irrigated. Later in the course of our interviews, I'll show him the famous scene as portrayed in the telemovie *Hawke*. He'll recoil, saying, 'Yeah, well, I did a lot of silly bloody things.')

Seeking a little illumination on what Hawke was like away from the gaze of the press, I visit significant figures in his life. Some are obvious choices: Kim Beazley, Gareth Evans, Ross Garnaut. Others less so: John Howard and John Singleton. My first stop, however, is the celebrated Australian diplomat Richard 'Dick' Woolcott, Hawke's friend for over fifty years.

Woolcott served under prime ministers Menzies, Holt, McEwan, Gorton, Whitlam, Fraser, Hawke and Keating. He was the third secretary for the Australian embassy in Moscow at the time of Stalin's death, Australia's high commissioner in Ghana, and ambassador to Indonesia, the Philippines and, later, the United Nations. Gough Whitlam called Woolcott 'Australia's leading diplomat for a generation ... he also possesses a great sense of humour from which even prime ministers were not spared.'

A sketch of Woolcott and his Danish-born wife Birgit – the epitome of the glamorous diplomat couple – would include their movie-star looks (he Cary Grant, she Anna Karina) and the fabulous parties, rich with conversation and gloss, held in embassies around the world.

Woolcott is eighty-nine years old and, a widower, lives alone in a Potts Point apartment building accessed down an alley and through multiple security doors. He greets me in a long-sleeved shirt, pants and socks, which he quickly apologises for.

An amalgam of two apartments, in a fifteen-storey building that sits atop the suburb's ridgeline, Woolcott's home has 180-degree views, taking in Woolloomooloo, the Opera House, the Sydney Harbour Bridge, Hyde Park and Sydney's puny skyline. A two-metre wide painting titled *New Australians Try to Light a Barbecue*, bought from the Australian artist Elaine Haxton for forty-five pounds sometime around 1954, fills a wall above a well-worn leather couch.

Woolcott is over six feet tall and slender, his good looks hardly diminished by age, his hair still with veins of black. He walks to a bureau and fishes through files before joining me on the balcony with a sheaf of photos: Bob and Dick with George Bush Senior; Dick and Bob and Gareth Evans peering worriedly at an out-of-frame television screen as Iraqi scuds rained on Israel during the 1991 Gulf War. Dick and Bob and others in tails before a dinner with Prince Charles and Princess Diana in 1989.

And so: What kind of man was Hawke? I ask.

'Well! Ha!' laughs Woolcott. 'When I first met him, he smoked heavily and drank heavily and I thought he was destined to go downhill. In those days, he was wild . . . Once, when I was ambassador in Indonesia, I was having a farewell party for the Austrian ambassador because he lived near me. And he wanted to have it in black tie. And I thought, *Christ, if you want to have it black tie, fine.*

'Well, Bob Hawke and Jim Ralston, who was from the left wing of the Labor Party, were visiting Jakarta to protest to the Indonesians about their policies towards East Timor. And I said to Hawke and Ralston, "Look, I've got this boring dinner. You're very welcome to come if you want to." And I thought they'd both say no but they turned up and, of course, they didn't have black tie, so I said, "I'll lend you formal Indonesian batik shirts." I put out these two shirts and they put the wrong ones on. Hawke was bursting out of his, while Ralston was swimming in the other.

'I remember the Austrian ambassador said to Hawke, "Mr Hawke, it's come to us from our embassy in Canberra that you're contemplating going into politics."

'Hawke banged down his pot of beer and looked at the Austrian ambassador and said, "YOU'RE LOOKING AT THE NEXT BLOODY PRIME MINISTER OF AUSTRALIA!" Now, I had grave doubts about that.'

How did the Austrian ambassador respond to the bombast?

'Oh, he was amazed!' says Woolcott. 'I often wonder what he reported back to Canberra. But it was not all that long after that Hawke gave up drinking . . .'

I mention that there seems to be two Hawkes: one playful, childlike, the other curt.

'He can be a bit curt. On this particular visit, Adam Malik was the Indonesian foreign minister and Hawke wanted to call on him, so I arranged it. And –' Woolcott laughs at the memory '– the treasurer was also in town, so I had to get somebody else to meet Bob and bring him to the foreign minister's house.

Anyway, I got there and saw no sign of Hawke or Richard, but all the dogs are barking. And they've come in the back way and are sitting there chatting away with Malik, the foreign minister. Malik says, "Well, I hope you've had a useful day, Mr Hawke. I believe you've called on the head of our trade unions." And Hawke says to him, "Your trade union movement is worth four-fifths of five-eighths of fuck-all!"

'Then he said to Malik, "You've been to the Philippines – you got any of those nice cigars that General Romulo has over there?" Malik says, "Yeah, I'll go upstairs and get one." Then Hawke, forgetting there were four Indonesian officials in suits who all spoke good English sitting nearby, turns around and says, "Amazing bloke, Malik. He used to be a fucking communist *and now he's working with this bastard Suharto!*" And Hawke ended up as prime minister! I thought that somebody who drank that much wouldn't be able to give it up like that, but he did. Completely. He didn't have an alcoholic drink for years.'

Still, for all his earthy charm, Woolcott says that as PM Hawke could be positively regal.

'I remember this one night at the Lodge in Canberra. The prime minister of Singapore at the time, Lee Kuan Yew, came through and Hawke was having a small dinner for him. I was there – because I was Secretary of Foreign Affairs, I suppose – and Bob lit up a cigar in front of Lee and blew out smoke and Lee Kwan Yew went –' Woolcott gesticulates wildly in front of his face '– "I CAN'T STAND SMOKE!"

'You'd expect Hawke would put it out. Instead, Hawke says to me, "Take him out to the courtyard." It's the middle of bloody winter! So I had to take Lee out into the courtyard while Bob finished his cigar. In those days, he very much did what he wanted to do.'

Did he ever receive you in the nude, as is the legend of pool-side cabinet meetings?

'I've heard those stories; I don't know whether they're true, although Churchill received Roosevelt in the bath. Maybe Hawke drew on that. Roosevelt went to see Churchill when he was in London and when he was shown in Churchill was in the bloody bath! Churchill said, "The British have nothing to hide from the Americans."'

Do you believe the secret to Hawke's success was the charismatic, friend-to-every-man persona?

'What is charismatic, but someone who attracts attention? I suppose so, yes. I've known all the prime ministers going back to Menzies and he was always, if he wanted to be, very engaging and happy to talk to people. He had that; he got on easily with people. That was a big advantage.'

Woolcott adds, 'A few years ago I was having a drink for my birthday. Here in Potts Point we're part of Wentworth, which is Malcolm Turnbull's electorate, so I asked Malcolm, I asked Bob Hawke – because I know him well – and I asked Tanya Plibersek. I didn't ask Keating, because Keating and Hawke don't get on.

'And I always remember, Hawke sat on the couch and was very relaxed and, pointing to Turnbull and Tanya Plibersek, he said, "Two future prime ministers of Australia are in the room!" And Turnbull, rather modestly, said, "Oh. Tanya might make it, but I don't think I ever will." Turnbull probably didn't mean it, of course.'

Woolcott recalls from his time as Secretary of Foreign Affairs that Hawke was open to 'sound advice' but would let you know, forcefully, if he believed you were wrong.

Were there any issues on which his opinion couldn't be swung?

'Yes, there's one. The 1989 Tasmanian state election. He took the view very strongly that Antarctica should be totally preserved. Now, there are no trees in Antarctica but he said, "No trees should be cut down!"' Woolcott belly laughs and says he argued that there was already a treaty that covered all that. 'But Hawke said, "No, no, no, we've got to go beyond what the treaty says." And that was essentially related to Tasmanian domestic policy.'

You mean to tell me, Mr Woolcott, that Hawke's successful quest to turn Antarctica into a natural reserve, devoted to peace and science for fifty years, for which he enlisted the iconic French underwater researcher Jacques Cousteau and French prime minister Michel Rocard, was primarily designed as a vote winner in the Tasmanian state election?

'Yeah, he felt that to demand that Antarctica be completely denuclearised and not used for any mineral excavation . . . it would appeal to the Labor Party in Tasmania.'

(When I repeat this to Hawke, he says Woolcott 'absolutely overstates the influence of the Tasmanian state election. It simply wasn't a factor in my decision. I'm telling you that as a fact!')

Political considerations aside, it's interesting, I tell Woolcott, that in an early exchange with Hawke about his legacy, he tells me that he rarely bites back at Keating's versions of history, but when Keating said that he was the first to broach the subject of locking up Antarctica, well, he *had to do something.*

'There's big argument about that,' says Woolcott. 'Hawke says that he was the first to talk to the French about it. Well he wasn't; Keating was . . . Bob would still deny that!'

How would Woolcott describe the dynamic between Hawke and Keating?

'Ah, well . . . it's still not all that good, because once Keating challenged him and won, Hawke never really forgave him for that. They still don't like each other.'

(To this, Hawke will later respond, 'Again, it's overstated. I have an *affection* for him.')

As someone who served them both, who was the better prime minister? 'Well, Keating was a very good treasurer and Hawke was a very good prime minister.'

How do they differ as men?

'Well, Keating was essentially a fairly conservative Catholic in many ways. Bob Hawke, while his father was a clergyman, was certainly less religious than Keating.'

And Hawke as prime minister, compared to Menzies?

'Bob was a better prime minister. I mean, Menzies was a good prime minister but he didn't have to deal with any real problems in those days . . .'

Still, I point out, there was Korea, 22 per cent inflation, the spectre of communism.

'Yeah, but life became more complicated later on and I thought Hawke handled the prime ministership better than *anybody* – certainly better than Malcolm Fraser. It was strange. Malcolm, he had control of both –' *Boom!* Woolcott slams his fist on the table for emphasis '– the Reps and the Senate –' *Boom!* '– and I've never known why he didn't use it. He could've been producing the reforms that Hawke and Keating did, but he didn't do it.'

And how about Hawke at eighty-six?

'I think he's gone downhill a bit in the last few months. He walks with a stick, he's a bit deaf in one ear, so it's not as easy to talk to him as it used to be. He keeps his hair in good shape, does a lot of *this* I've noticed . . .' Woolcott pats his hair theatrically. 'And some people think he's vain . . .'

Is Hawke vain?

'Well, he's interested in how he looks, but he's not necessarily vain. He certainly likes to keep himself looking tidy.'

Woolcott says if he had to describe Hawke to someone who didn't know him, he would say he was 'a guy who had the capacity once he set –' *Boom!* The fist comes down again '– the goal –'

Boom! '– of going into politics, of becoming a prime minister, he did everything he needed to do to achieve that.'

And he'll be remembered well?

'Hawke showed that he could give up the grog and perform as prime minister. It was an amazing act of survival.'

— CHAPTER 6 —

FINDING LOVE THROUGH INFIDELITY

PERSISTENT RAIN. A SALLY BACK AND FORTH WITH A partially deaf former prime minister on the intercom. Hawke has been given the duty of vetting guests as Blanche trains with Ryan Barraclough, the champion rower turned personal trainer whose calves I'll be invited to comment on later.

Hello?

Eh?

Bob!

Who is it?

Derek!

Eh?

The front gate, which is on the third level, is wedged open. I forget the intercom and walk in. It ain't exactly Fort Knox here. But, then, security has never been on the top of Hawke's requirements.

When the Palestinian journalist Munif Mohammed Abou Rish plotted to assassinate Hawke in 1974 over his support for Israel (Munif was killed by Israeli security forces before he could complete the hit), Hawke refused to hide behind a phalanx of bodyguards.

John Singleton says that when he gave Hawke the keys to his Birchgrove house in 1991 after his pal had lost the leadership, 'he probably slipped the guard a hundred bucks to fuck off. Bob was never one for security. He had whatever he had to have.'

I see more of the Northbridge house this time. On a raised platform on the second level is a jarrah dining table that seats twelve, probably fourteen at a pinch. Custom-made by an Italian craftsman, it has hosted various Chinese businessmen, Arab sheiks, Rhodes Scholars, politicians and American billionaires.

A vertical aquarium is built into a wall and multi-coloured tropical fish languidly flap up and down. There's a photograph stuck to the fridge called *Bob on Toast*; taken by the Sydney photographer Simon Bernhardt, it shows Hawke holding a slice of toast smeared with Vegemite under his nose, his brilliantined hair glossy under studio lighting. Also affixed to the fridge is a small sculpture of lips in chains by Hawke's stepson Louis.

On a banquette in an informal dining area that opens to the second-floor terrace is a copy of *Capital in the Twenty-First Century,* a book on economic inequality by the French economist Thomas Piketty. Hawke made his reputation in 1958 as an advocate for the ACTU, winning an unheard of fifteen-shilling increase in the basic wage. Piketty beats a similar tambourine.

'When the rate of return on capital exceeds the rate of growth of output and income,' writes Piketty, 'capitalism automatically generates arbitrary and unsustainable inequalities that radically undermine the meritocratic values on which democratic societies are based.'

Hawke was schooled in inequality when he visited India for the 1952 World Christian Youth Conference.

'And it was Christmas,' Hawke had told me in an earlier interview. 'There was this big feast put on at the home of one of the wealthy Christians there. I remember they were singing, *The world to Christ we bring. Christ to the world we bring. The world to Christ we bring.* They were in this palatial place, big gates, and all these poverty-stricken Indians were hanging on the gate and looking in.' Hawke shook his head. 'I thought, my god, this is ridiculous. So I left the feast and went back to my digs and got some warm clothing I had and came back and found a couple of kids sleeping out in the open who were obviously very uncomfortable. I gave them the clothing and left.'

In 1987, more than half a million Australian kids lived at or below what constituted the poverty line. At his campaign launch at the Sydney Opera House that year, Hawke famously (over)promised: 'By 1990 no Australian child will be living in poverty . . .' It was an impossible, reckless pledge, even with the raft of benefits the government would soon pay via rent assistance, family benefit and a child disability allowance.

Still, 'A number of women came up to me in the street with tears in their eyes and told me it made all the difference in their lives,' says Hawke.

The printed speech actually read 'no Australian child *need* live in poverty'. But Hawke being Hawke – Brotherhood of Man and so on – left out the qualifier. He was Australia's master communicator, after all. He would prevail.

He didn't. Twenty years later it was three-quarters of a mill.

Still, he feels that poverty and its effects are catastrophic. An unequal distribution of wealth, he says now, is the root cause of terrorism and Europe's dramatic swing to the far right.

On the Palestinians: 'You've got to create an economically viable Palestinian state. You've got no jobs, no growth. Young people are going to be attracted to violence.'

On the west's swing to the right: 'The situation in America is frightful, and in a lot of other countries. Unless people feel they're getting, in the Australian idiom, a fair go, they're going to find it attractive to follow those who get up and preach extremes. Creating a fair society is the *sine qua non* for dealing with these sorts of problems.'

In his 1994 memoir Hawke wrote, 'Unashamedly, I love Australia with a passionate intensity.'

Why?

Because 'the fair-go concept is not just words,' Hawke will tell me. 'It's still part of the Australian ethos – perhaps not burning as brightly as it did earlier, but people are regarded on their merits, not where they were born, what level they are on the socioeconomic structure.

'This is real. We were amongst the earliest movers in the world in decent legislation regarding the women's vote and pensions and social welfare provisions. They're much more part of the Australian ethos than in so many other countries. The concept of the rule of law, some of the very good things we've got from our British heritage, and parliamentary democracy, all that's been enlarged and strengthened culturally, and with cultural enrichment that's come with the influx of people from overseas. I don't think it can be said too often that the transition and the ethnic composition of Australia has been, in terms of the scale of it, the most peaceful anywhere in history.'

And now, on a July afternoon in Sydney, a cold south-west wind whips the back of the old patriot's house. But here on the terrace, with the sun sparkling off the white hulls of the yachts below, it could be August in Antibes.

Hawke wears a white shirt and striped tie, a Nike jacket and fitted grey sweatpants. The tie's a leftover from a lunch event at which American vice-president Joe Biden spoke on the US–Australian alliance.

He greets me with the now-familiar: 'Did you bring a cigar?'

It's warm enough, but Bob switches on the outdoor heater. He cuts the new cigar (Romeo y Julieta, from Cuba, $22).

Small talk. Attempts at lighting with a plastic lighter.

You like going to functions?

'Not particularly. The one I went to today, they were the best part of two hours late . . . *oh fuck –*' the cigar doesn't light '– and not a word of apology.'

The flint is worn. Hawke grabs a box of matches.

How was the speech?

'It was a good speech. But the welcoming applause was less than overwhelming. People were *shitty!*'

Is America still our greatest friend?

'I guess,' he says. 'It's got so many weaknesses, but it's still our most important ally. As far as the relationship between America and China, it's absolutely crucial. That's why one of the reasons is that apart from the intrinsics of the Israel–Palestine dispute, if we could get them working together on something like that, that would be a hell of a good thing for the relationship generally.'

At this point, Blanche brings the couple's trainer to meet me. Earlier, she'd told me about a whale-shaped foam device called an 'Oov' that had been delivering fantastic results. The Oov extends the spine during exercise, which stimulates 'healthy intervertebral disc lubrication'.

I mention I've also seen a VibroGym in the house, a vibrating platform whose high-speed up-and-down movements promise 'a tremendous amount of muscle activity'.

'I hate it,' says Blanche.

Hawke is wounded. 'Why did you decide you hated the VibroGym?'

'I hate it. You know I never go on it.'

'I didn't know you hated it.'

Blanche and the trainer leave for her afternoon's workout.

Hawke draws hard on the Romeo y Julieta. It's my signal to begin.

I want to talk about the joy of love. Last week, when I asked about your dream of happiness, you spoke about the joy you have found with Blanche.

'It's just impossible to describe adequately the happiness that we get from our relationship,' he says. 'It's a paradox in one sense. We share a number of interests and we also have divergent interests, which is a recipe for a good relationship, because you can learn from the interests of your partner. And in the things that you really share an interest in, you can spend a lot of time talking and considering those issues. To be specific, we're both very interested in politics, domestic and international politics. And we spend a lot of time talking about these issues, watching television together on political subjects. There are those shared interests which bring you together, and then . . . Blanche's writing is something which gives her enormous fulfilment . . . I know I'm terribly proud of her qualities as a writer and the commitment she exhibits in producing her books. While we don't talk at length and in detail, she always gives me early drafts to look at, so I have an involvement.'

Of course, this was the first woman you'd met who wanted to talk about the machinations of wage-fixing within the Arbitration Commission.

'*Intelligently*,' emphasises Hawke. 'This is on the non-sexual side of things, the interests; it's very important to have the shared interests and the difference in interests. That's something that is very important in our relationship. Of course, we have just been physically attracted to one another from the very first time we met at that engagement in Jakarta.'

When you have the great physical attraction matched with a

great intellectual attraction, is that when you think those great loves develop?

'Physical attraction is one thing, and it's a fairly common thing,' he says, 'but to have a huge physical attraction associated with intellectual companionship is extraordinarily stimulating.'

Blanche said that after meeting you, and when you started a relationship, that everything shimmered with life and more life, I tell him. She writes, 'Researching was a joy. Writing was a joy. Everything was a joy.' Was it obvious, the effect you had on her?

'Well, it was mutual. It wasn't just my effect on her. It was a mutual effect and we lifted one another.'

You've obviously read *On Longing*, Blanche's book on your great affair. She describes your life at the time as a 'freewheeling, decentralised harem with four or five favourites, and a shoe-sale queue of one-night stands'.

Was that true? Were you really that much of a stud?

'Well, it's not entirely *untrue*,' says Hawke echoing an interview with Michael Parkinson, who asked on his eponymous television show if the *National Times*' claim that he 'performs like a playboy' was true.

'I have my moments,' Hawke had said with a grin to rapturous applause.

Now, he does supply the caveat: 'But I think she's taken it to the limit.'

In 1978, I say, you told her that you had been struggling to choose between your Swiss lover, nicknamed Paradiso, and Blanche. You had a dream that they were both on a roulette wheel and when the wheel was spun the ball came to land on Blanche. You took that as a sign that you were meant to marry her. Do you remember that dream?

'Just vaguely,' Hawke replies, dodging. 'I can't make much of that.'

Then, in 1979, you broke off the relationship. How was your emotional state at the time when you decided to split?

'I was extraordinarily upset. I was on the verge of making the decision about moving into parliament and ... divorce from the marriage would not have been an optimal sort of thing to be doing at that point. It was an extraordinarily difficult decision that I took.'

How hard was it to cut off the woman you love and not make contact?

'Extremely difficult. It was obviously terribly difficult for Blanche ...'

Hawke's voice trails off.

Did you find it hard knowing that she would eventually see other men?

'No, I had a totally full life. While the memories were there, I had an enormous amount to occupy my mind and my time.'

In November 1988, you called her. Why?

'She'd never really been out of my mind,' says Hawke. 'I just felt I'd love to see her again.'

In *On Longing,* Blanche describes their first touch in a decade.

He suggested a time, a place and a way – an exercise that was now excruciatingly tricky, since wherever he went he was under guard and accompanied by officials, not every one of whom he trusted. We met in a confidant's house in Sydney, both very nervous – but then we rushed into each other's arms, laughing. We laughed at ourselves, and with delight and with relief that we still loved each other. Our happiness was intensified by the imaginative solutions we had to find to be able to meet: a red wig, a stetson, the kindness of friends. We knew we each had other lovers, and we were not going to be foolish a second time.

'It was just marvellous to be with her again,' says the more prosaic Hawke.

Shortly after, while on assignment for the *New York Times* in northern Queensland, the seven-seater plane Blanche was on crashed into the Pacific. Blanche was uninjured but the phone call to Hawke from the pair's 'discreet social secretary' was crushing.

'Blanche has been in a plane crash,' he told Hawke.

'Oh my god!' Hawke gasped.

At that moment, he felt as if his world had evaporated. The great love of his life . . . *gone*. As Hawke would later tell Blanche, he felt as if he'd died.

Beat.

'But she's alright,' said the go-between.

'Devastating,' he says now. 'He really was a drama queen. Not telling me straight out'.

What do you believe the keys are to a successful marriage?

'To respect one another. I mean, I admire her. She admires me. It's not just a physical thing,' says Hawke. 'Of course that's there. And it's a strong part of it. But we genuinely respect one another and we're interested in what one another's doing. I have tremendous admiration for her, at her age, she's still writing an historical quartet. Fabulous.'

Do you think we're mature enough as a society to talk about affairs that turn into great loves? About the potential to find true and enduring love through infidelity?

Hawke abruptly shifts gears.

Gone is the lover lost in a waterfall of memory. Even nearly five decades since he first met Blanche, and a quarter of a century since he went public with it, Hawke instinctively knows the concept of finding love through infidelity is a concept few would be able to grasp.

'I don't want to talk about it very much,' he says. 'These are things which are very intimate and personal.'

It's hard to argue with that. Once Hawke revealed his affair with Blanche and they confessed their overwhelming love, a triumph of passion over pragmatism, the pair had their heads kicked by the Australian press.

The nadir was *60 Minutes*, supposedly the high-water mark of serious journalism, with journalist Charles Wooley asking the pair when they first had sex. Was it before or after Hawke had ended his marriage to Hazel?

Now, twenty years on, the show returns for Bob and Blanche redux, this time with a two-part celebration of the pair's enduring relationship. Perversely, the old scandal becomes the new interview's hook, the publicity surrounding its broadcast reminding viewers:

> At sixty-four, the former prime minister had announced his separation from his wife of forty years, Hazel, and publicly declared his love for the much-younger Blanche. It was the biggest romantic scandal in Australian political history, with the public turning on our most popular prime minister. Hawke shifted from much-loved leader of the nation to one half of Australia's most recognised and scrutinised 'two-timing couple'.

Wooley is once again assigned to the story. He takes the opportunity to amend history and ask what he believes is a much better question.

> Wooley: I must say now with the weight of experience and the years upon me, I wouldn't ask when it began but rather how long can it last?
>
> Bob: Forever!

Blanche: Absolutely! I think the thing for both of us is love means adoration.

Wooley: You're a believer in romantic love?

Blanche: Yes, I'm a believer in something a bit more than romantic love because as we understand it now it's somewhat saccharine.

Redemption? Or just a bone thrown to an old philanderer guaranteed to light up the show's ratings?

When Hazel died in 2013, the *Sydney Morning Herald* was still plying the 'brave-wife, wanton-lover' narrative:

> . . . hovering off stage like some lipsticked wraith was the other woman, Blanche d'Alpuget. Australians knew all this but kept a sort of conspiracy of silence. Instead, as Hazel stood by her man with pluck and grace, people took her to their hearts in a manner never extended to any other prime minister's wife. Perhaps it was her very vulnerability that made Hazel so beloved.

Lipsticked wraith! It's such a hoary old line I express my delight to Blanche via email, who responds: *Lipsticked wraith! My god, where do you find these things?*

It isn't hard.

Despite her bona fides as a noted writer, as a journalist whose non-fiction work centred on the very unsexy role of trade unions in Australia, Blanche is cast in the country's cultural history as the dumb, painted whore to Hazel Hawke's elegant Madonna.

After Blanche's book *Hawke: The Prime Minister* was released in 2011, the popular columnist Miranda Devine wrote a piece titled, 'A Slap in the Face of History'. Devine claimed Blanche stole Hazel's dream and rewrote Bob's history to diminish her contribution. 'Bob and Hazel also had a love story, and in Blanche's book it was trivialised as a mere bond of convenience,' she wrote.

After the pair appear on *60 Minutes*, the mailbag is swollen three-to-one against the lovers.

In the following week's episode, reporter Peter Overton appears on the television screen to introduce viewers' comments.

> **It's said if you want a dinnertime, ding-dong, no-holds barred argument, then just talk politics, religion or . . . sex. Which brings us to your rather ferocious comments about last week's story with Bob Hawke, our agnostic former prime minister who left his wife for . . .**

(Overton stares mournfully into the camera lens; gravitas pulses from the screen)

> **. . . another woman.**

Cue short version of episode.

> **Charles Wooley thought Bob and Blanche's love story was charming, but at home you have *long memories*.**

> *Bob's betrayal of Hazel all those years ago is never forgotten.* Karin, Facebook

---

> *This couple is the Australian version of Charles and Camilla. They make me sick.* Tracey, Facebook

---

There is an interlude showing vintage footage of Blanche rubbing sun cream over Bob's pectorals and into the upper delta of his hams and loins.

'I like that!' says Bob.

Cue excerpt from episode:

> Wooley: Blanche, you were portrayed at times as the scarlet woman. In fact, nothing could be further from the truth.
>
> Blanche: That's right. The fact that I was a writer with a career, and an international career, was simply airbrushed out of the picture. And I was portrayed as Bob's much younger trophy wife.

Back to the viewers' response:

> Overton: And still, the outrage flowed.

> *Thanks for glamorising extramarital affairs* 60 Minutes. Suzi, Facebook

---

> Overton: But then . . .

> *All these people casting judgement. What's the saying? Let he who hasn't sinned cast the first stone.* Maya, Facebook

---

It's a fine sentiment – even if it is the minority view. For public and private morality are two very different creatures. The celebrity or notable is held to an impossibly pious ideal, while the viewer, whose life is never scrutinised by camera or reporter, can cavort freely.

Hawke's old pal Colin Cunningham told him if he ever left Hazel he'd be hated by every damn female in Australia.

'Well, that was a fact,' says Col. 'I sat down with him and he said, "I'm leaving Hazel," and I said, "Oh Jesus, you'll be *hated* now. Women will just fucken ... *hate* ... you." He said, "Colin, I don't care. I've been hated before." He said, "I'm going to spend the next twenty years with the woman I love." And that was that.'

Because you can't keep the lid on a beautiful love story.

'Yeah, and he's just the same now as if it happened yesterday! I mean, who's like that? Ah, Jesus, it's sickening. If you go out he's holding hands with her, walking down the street and all this. I've got a good wife but *holding hands*? Oh, he's bloody embarrassing at times!' Col snorts. 'He's just infatuated with the woman. That's all. Yeah. *Infatuated.*

'He'd take a bullet for her. Fair dinkum. If someone fired a gun at her he'd jump in front of the bullet.'

— CHAPTER 7 —

ON SONIA
AND ISLAM

WITH THE DOOR TO HIS GREAT LOVE AFFAIR CLOSED, I present the previous day's news to Hawke for examination.

The TV host Sonia Kruger had said on the talk show *Today* that she wanted Australia's borders closed to Muslim immigrants; she said she wanted to feel safe when she celebrated Australia Day.

It's the sort of talk that kills Hawke. He helped establish the International Centre for Muslim and non-Muslim Understanding in South Australia and believes one of the great dangers confronting the world is the lack of understanding in regards to the Muslim world.

What would you say to someone like Ms Kruger, shaken by the notion of Muslims at the gate? I ask.

First, Hawke calls Kruger's posit 'frightful' and says it's a little rough to start closing the door to 'a nation which has been built on immigration'. He believes in a sturdy and non-discriminatory immigration policy. Curtin's decision to open the door to the world, says Hawke, is why we punch above our weight.

'This has *made* Australia. It's strengthened us economically and culturally enriched us. For people to be speaking against any nationality, race, creed and religion is a contradiction to what Australia is about. I just wish that these people would sit down and think about it more rationally. There's no doubt that fanatical Muslims are dangerous. So are fanatical Christians. So are fanatical Jews. I was talking to a Jewish friend of mine relatively recently and he was going on about the –'

Suddenly, Blanche appears from behind a sliding door, clearly post-workout given the sheen on her cheek, and squeezes her hands along the length of her husband's trapezius.

'Who's this beautiful thing?' says Hawke, leaning into his wife's still-enviable chest, his face turned upwards.

So, your Jewish friend, I remind him.

'He was attacking Muslims and I said, "You mustn't do that." Fanatical Muslims are obviously to be despised and dealt with. I said, "I just ask you to remember one thing: it wasn't a fanatical Muslim who murdered the Israeli prime minister [Yitzhak Rabin] – it was a fanatical Jew. It was the fanatical right-wing Christians in America who encouraged Bush to go into Iraq." As I said, it's the fanaticism of any religion which is a danger. Islam has been a great religion over the centuries; they've been able to live peaceably with other religions. And we've just got to do all that we can, political leaders and ordinary people, to be open and discuss issues and reject fanaticism from wherever it comes.'

Kruger also said, 'It's vital a democratic society be able to discuss these sorts of issues without being labelled a racist.' It's a reasonable request, I suggest.

'Well, just to shout "racist" is not appropriate,' says Hawke. 'We should condemn those who act racially themselves. But we don't achieve anything by being counter-racist – racist the other way. I hold the view that we are all brothers and sisters, and people must be dealt with on their merits, not on the basis of some prejudiced, preconceived notion about the religion to which they belong or belief that they hold.'

Still, I push, in light of attacks in New York, Bali, Jakarta, Madrid, London, Nice, Orlando, San Bernardino, Paris, Berlin and Sydney, and beheadings on the streets of London to a church in Normandy to an Ikea in Västerås, Sweden, as well as the myriad bombings in Iraq, Jordan and beyond, not to mention the Shia–Sunni conflict, can you understand why people might feel as if the levers of government were being pulled without due acknowledgement of their concerns?

'Of course I can understand why people are concerned. Any sensible person is concerned about the dangerous state of the world,' says Hawke. 'In the Cold War, which was a very dangerous period, you had the situation where your enemy was in identified areas. You knew where they were. With terrorists, the opposite is true. You also had the distinction that the Russians didn't want to die themselves. For the terrorists, on the contrary, they think death is glorious, so you've got a much more difficult situation . . . This is all the more reason why we should call upon people to behave decently and rationally, and not on the basis of prejudice. I can't say it more clearly than that.'

But Hawke says there isn't a damn thing anyone can do about Islamic terrorism until Israel and Palestine are two separate states.

'That's why I'm working with the Chinese to try to get them to talk about it,' he says.

He's referred to this idea briefly before, but now I ask him to expand on it.

'Well, I'm very close to the Chinese and to their top security and intelligence people. I've said to them that now that they have to take a real interest in the Middle East. They had the Israeli prime minister and the head of the Palestinian Authority there in China. I've urged the Chinese . . . to offer to sit down with the Americans in talks with Israel and Palestine, because it's my judgement it would change the chemistry of the situation.'

According to Hawke, the Palestinians and the Arabs don't trust the Americans to be impartial. The Arab world sees the US as protectors of Israel and not much else. But China is a superpower without a stake in the game, apart from spreading its wings economically.

'If you had China and the United States acting as negotiators, there would be a very real chance of getting a result, and that's what I urge them to do . . . It would change the chemistry entirely,' Hawke says, adding he's 'been in touch' with Hillary Clinton to push his idea.

'When she becomes president, as I believe she will, I'll talk to her about it,' he says.

What are the steps to achieving a solution to the Israel–Palestine question and what does that solution look like? I ask. More to the point, why would a Hawke plan succeed when everyone from Kissinger to Clinton has failed miserably?

'Well, just two or three things. Firstly, as part of the resolution, both China and America together should say to the parties that they are committed to creating an economically viable Palestinian state. You've got no jobs, no growth. Young people are just going to be attracted to violence, so I've formulated many years ago what I call the Powell Plan for Palestine. This was when Colin Powell was the Secretary of State. He supported it absolutely.'

The PPP, says Hawke, was a twenty-first-century version of America's Marshall Plan, whereby the equivalent of $120 billion (in 2016 dollars) was pumped into Europe after World War II – to rebuild the joint, sure, but mostly to stave off the influence of the Soviet Union.

'Western Europe was very much in danger of falling to the Communists, so the Marshall Plan poured money into Western Europe to revive their economies. It was one of the great acts of statesmanship,' says Hawke.

In 2003, Hawke, along with Blanche, even met with then chairman of the PLO Yasser Arafat at his Ramallah compound to sell the idea.

As Blanche describes in *Hawke: The Prime Minister*:

A pall of misery and despair hung over the towns and villages of the West Bank in the autumn of 2003. The few food shops that were open had scant supplies: limp carrots, tinned milk, some apples, bags of rice. Israel was already building the Separation Wall . . . Hawke was driven on to Ramallah, which seemed a ghost town. There was a high wall around Arafat's compound and Israeli soldiers on top of all the buildings that overlooked it. Inside the compound a number of buildings had been bombed and lay in ruins, as did the entrance to Arafat's house. Hawke was ushered through khaki canvas flats, which now served as a door, up a flight of stairs where a wardrobe and sandbags covered a bomb-hole in the wall. Hawke had detested Arafat for decades as the embodiment of violence. It was only his conviction that the international situation was increasingly dangerous that had brought him this far.

The chairman of the Palestinian Authority had been the world's foremost political trickster for more than thirty years, its Great Survivor, the Br'er Rabbit of international affairs: smart, cunning, funny, charming, lucky. And a killer. But when he entered dressed in his military uniform, surrounded by aides, he was a pitiful figure, a warlord defeated, depressed and enervated. The dream he had pursued for decades lay in rubble.

And yet here was Bob Hawke, a former prime minister of Australia and great friend to Israel, offering hope, a way out of the dirt.

'I expounded the Powell Plan concept to him,' says Hawke. 'And he was very, very positively responsive. I said to him that he would have to understand that the attacks on Israel would have to cease and I said everyone will understand that you can't absolutely control every single person, but you'd have to use your influence to stop those attacks. I said also, you'd have to understand that the huge amounts of money that are going to be involved cannot be handled directly by you. It must be handled independently so there's no corruption, and all the money is used for the right purposes. I mentioned Jim Wolfensohn, who was then president of the World Bank, and a good friend of mine over many years. Arafat said yes, he knew Wolfensohn and respected him, and then he absolutely agreed to that.'

Of course, shortly after his meeting with Arafat, the Bush government bulldozed Iraq and had neither the international capital nor the energy to lead a two-state solution.

'Colin [Powell] is a lovely man,' says Hawke. 'He said, "Bob, I supported your plan entirely but I couldn't get them to talk about anything but Iraq."'

Six months after our discussion, to coincide with the visit of Israel's prime minister Benjamin 'Bibi' Netanyahu to Australia, Hawke will write a piece in the *Australian Financial Review* calling for a renewed focus on Palestinian statehood.

'I will always remember my meeting immediately after the end of the Yom Kippur War in October 1973 with the then Prime Minister Golda Meir,' Hawke wrote.

I listened with admiration and in total agreement as this wonderful woman, still traumatised with grief, looked into

my eyes and said there could be no peace for Israel until there was an honourable settlement of the aspirations of the Palestinian people . . . the situation is clear – starkly clear. Like the Jews in the Soviet Union and the blacks in South Africa, the Palestinians have an aspiration to be fully free. But with a majority of the Netanyahu Government openly declared against a Palestinian state they understandably see little hope in the political process . . . Is there not emerging the danger of Israel being blinded to the threat to its very soul and the vision of its future?

Bibi will reply, 'What kind of state will it be that they are advocating? A state that calls for Israel's destruction? A state whose territory will be used immediately for radical Islam?'

Those on the right, and even the centre-left, will line up to take a swing.

The Victorian Labor MP Michael Danby accuses Hawke, and Rudd and Evans, of trying to smash the ALP's relationship with Israel. 'I might say to all of the heroes who are beating up on a country, a democratic country where there are gay pride parades – there aren't any in the surrounding countries – or Christmas celebrations – there aren't any in the surrounding countries – why don't they beat up on China when the Chinese president comes to Australia?' Mr Danby told Sky News. 'Where is Bob Carr, Gareth Evans and Bob Hawke when the terrible things that are happening in Tibet are discussed? They never raise their heads, they never raise their heads to power. They want to try and provoke the Israeli prime minister and upset relations between him and the Labor Party prior to Netanyahu's visit.'

The Australian's foreign affairs writer Greg Sheridan describes Hawke, Rudd and Gareth Evans as a 'caterwauling coven of craven zeitgeist whisperers . . . intoning sterile incantations' like the three witches from Macbeth, to no end other than the affirmation of their own supreme virtue. Referring to Hawke and Rudd in particular, Sheridan claims they 'are always keen to lavish themselves with praise and moral credentials they simply do not possess.'

Hawke, of course, has been a defender of Israel's right to exist, and flourish, since 1971, when he was invited to deliver the inaugural Sam Cohen Memorial Lecture, named for Victorian senator Sam Cohen, who founded the Jewish Council to Combat Fascism and Anti-Semitism in 1942.

Hawke recalls: 'I went over [to Israel] and I was very taken by the Histadrut, which is a trade union movement there. They were very strong within the Labor Party and within politics there. The Israelis were extraordinarily impressive in terms of the enthusiasm with which they were going about the creation of a new state based upon social, democratic principles, and the thought of them being destroyed after being created by the act of the United Nations was appalling to me. So I identified with their right to exist as an independent nation.'

It's a remarkable joint, I say. They've turned that little slice of dirt and rock into such a prosperous democracy.

'Yeah,' says Hawke, enthusiasm deflating abruptly. 'But we've got to recognise it's got some blind spots too. Some of its treatment of the Arab people has been less than brilliant. As I say, I've always maintained a commitment to the rights of the Palestinians to their own state, but not at the expense of the destruction to Israel.'

Still, says, Hawke, it's important for friends to be open to criticism. To slam Hawke as anti-Israel is a gross misreading of history. Hawke was the man who, as ALP president, bit back when Whitlam steered his government to what he called an 'even-handed' approach to the Israelis and the plight of the Palestinians.

In diplomatic cables published by Wikileaks, it is revealed that Hawke told a confidant of the US embassy that Whitlam had an 'immoral, unethical and ungrateful' approach to the Israelis and that he'd 'caved in' on the question for 'commercial reasons'. Whitlam, in return, regarded Hawke as a 'pro-Israel fanatic'.

With the current surge of Islamic terrorism, I ask, are we at the beginning of a long conflict or do you see light at the end of such a dark tunnel?

Hawke contemplates the question. Looks at his cigar. Draws. Releases smoke.

'No one can honestly say that they know the answer to that,' he says at last. 'What we do know are that the sorts of things that need to be done to resolve the Palestinian/Israeli issues are critically important. Then we need political leadership. I'm hopeful that with the election of Hillary, we'll have someone who is absolutely committed. I'm not saying this wanting to denigrate Obama, but I don't think he's provided the sort of dynamic leadership that's required. I still hope that leaders will emerge who will realise what's got to be done, and who are committed to creating fairer societies so that the extremists don't have such fertile ground as they do at the present time.'

Hawke says one of the great problems facing the west is that there isn't a lot of leadership talent out there, least of all someone with the intellectual and political weight to machete through a thicket of contradictions like the Israel–Palestine question.

'Not one outstanding leader in the democracies anywhere in the world today,' he says.

Merkel?

'If you listed all the past German chancellors, she'd probably come in fifth or sixth.'

Trump?

Hawke pauses, contemptuously blows a ball of smoke.

'Certainly not Trump.'

Historically, has there been anyone else like Donald Trump in your life?

'No, not within the major democracies that I can recall.' This, he says, is a new phenomenon of modern American politics. Hawke unleashes even more smoke, furious now.

'Gah! Don't talk to me about Donald Trump. This bloke's *insane.*'

Should we fret? Do we stand on the precipice of a new dark age?

'Trump's not going to become president,' Hawke reassures. 'He's just a passing aberration.'

— CHAPTER 8 —

KIM BEAZLEY

T HE THREE-TIME LEADER OF THE OPPOSITION AND former deputy prime minister of Australia stoops over the concierge desk of a mid-range Sydney hotel, his six-foot-two frame dwarfing staff in their black Nehru jackets.

His tone is polite, although firm enough to indicate inaction on a requested room change won't be tolerated. As unseen screens are examined and keys tapped, Mr Kim Beazley, AC, leans on one elbow and fiddles with his telephone.

Is there a better way to survey a man than as an unseen observer at close quarters? For a public figure who was as famous for his sartorial inelegance (one former employee at the Department of Defence described Beazley to me as 'a man who eats his dinner off his shirt') as his inability to prise John Howard off the prime ministerial throne, he presents well in navy blazer, clean white shirt and the sort of boots a farmer might wear on his first trip to the big smoke.

Eventually, I reveal myself.

'Mr Beazley?'

Beazley spins around to shake my hand. 'Oh, hello. *Hello!*'

he says, in a bright voice closer to pre-teen than pre-retirement.

He follows me into a large anteroom to talk about his great friend and mentor, Bob Hawke.

We sit a foot or so apart, Beazley on a two-seat microfibre couch, me on a bamboo chair with an angled seat. It's only a determination to avoid embarrassment and the strength in my hams that stops me from sliding onto the tiled floor.

Beazley, who is almost sixty-eight, has small blue eyes and grey hair, which is full enough at this late stage of the game, and he pats it down at regular intervals. His skin appears untouched by the Western Australian sun, a legacy of decades spent in Canberra's gloom.

Hawke and Beazley revel in their commonalities. Both are Rhodes Scholars, both from politically significant Western Australian families: Hawke's Uncle Bert was state premier and Beazley's father the federal Minister for Education during Whitlam's abbreviated reign.

The pair's first encounter was at a meeting of the Labor National Executive in 1971, Beazley drawn to the Labor Party for its opposition to the Vietnam War.

Nine years later, they were both elected members of parliament for the first time. In 1983, Hawke became prime minister and appointed Beazley his Minister for Aviation.

As Hawke recalls, 'In a sort of surrogate way, I almost thought of him as a son. And I, I suppose, took him under my wing, in a sense. Had to have a pretty big wing. Pretty big bloke.'

Beazley, in turn, adored – adores – Hawke.

He was in London ('on one of those parliamentary jollies' with John Dawkins, who'd become Hawke's first Minister for Finance), when he learned that Fraser had called an early election in the expectation of facing Bill Hayden, not the immensely popular Hawke.

'Fraser only found out about [the leadership change] a second before he had to stand up and make the statements he did about the calling of the election,' says Beazley. 'One fellow described to me as Fraser opened the press conference, "That rustling noise you heard was Fraser's trousers hitting the ground." He ... was *gone*. Fraser knew it. He was gone the moment Hawke was leader.'

Beazley rocks back and forth as he recalls a panicked woman from Australia's High Commission in London visiting him and Dawkins at their hotel because they'd changed their flights in order to return to Australia earlier than anticipated.

'You poor men!' she cried. 'Your party has changed its leader and the other side has ambushed you and this is a terrible thing, to have to go home early and face such a conundrum.'

'What do you mean?' chortled Beazley. 'We're both going home to be ministers.'

It's important to point out, says Beazley, that unlike a lot of political leaders, Hawke wasn't driven to office for fame or power for power's sake.

'Listen,' he says, 'a lot of people want to be prime minister. A lot of people would take the view that they should be or could be, but Bob never had that ambition without combining it with a program. He said, "I want to be prime minister not because I'm a golden son or because I have any entitlement, but because I stand for these things." His strengths were, overwhelmingly, a very clear-cut view of what he wanted to do with the country. He wasn't wandering around vaguely looking for an agenda. His experience at the ACTU meant that when he got into parliament, he didn't regard it necessarily as the be-all and end-all of democracy. It was important, but the democracy was broader than just parliament. Democracy involved an ongoing consultation with the Australian people beyond simply election times. The British nineteenth-century political theorist Walter

Bagehot once said that the great prime ministers are men of commonplace opinions and uncommon administrative abilities. That was Bob. If the majority of the community didn't feel that way then Bob would convert them to the view that they always had felt that way and by appealing to their better instincts.'

Hawke's gift was an ability to use his natural intellect, tutored at Oxford and honed inside Australia's arbitration courts, combined with his everyman persona, to shift public attitudes that might've seemed, to a lesser man, bolted on.

'The guy was ultra-charisma,' says Beazley. 'He always looked to Australians like the quintessential Aussie bloke and talked like the quintessential Aussie bloke. They trusted and listened to him. And he used it relentlessly in areas where Australians have always been ultra-sensitive. They've always been ultra-sensitive on the subject of immigration. Bob really sold the non-discrimination policy. Where many Australians were very reluctant to engage on the South African apartheid issue, Bob goes head-on and sets up the Eminent Persons Group that plays a major role in the transitioning in South Africa from white rule to majority rule.

'Then he sees that the Australian economy can't survive, that our market's too small in our ultra-protected cocoon. It's not publicly popular, but he gets out there and he argues his convictions. He always did the Australian public the honour of assuming that they had intelligence. He was the quintessential democrat as a political figure.'

Another important trait of the Hawke government, according to Beazley, was . . . wait for it . . . a deep trust of bureaucracy – a belief that the public service was there to serve whomever is in power and not to be flattered or terrorised.

One week into the Hawke government, ministers were told to jettison their chiefs of staff into lesser roles and to find an existing bureaucrat – the same bureaucrats who'd worked for Fraser's Liberal government for eight years – to run their ministries.

'We are not going to make a mess of this government,' Hawke told the ministers. 'We need to have a government that is an orderly, disciplined process of getting policy to the cabinet and policy to the public. You're not going to do that off the back of people who have no experience in doing it.'

'Everyone's jaw hit the floor,' says Beazley. 'But he had a really deep respect for the public service and what it was capable of delivering. He didn't care about the fact that it had worked for a long time for Liberal governments; his view was that they're public servants and that's what they do. It was another strength, that trust.'

The trust extended to his cabinet.

'You look at leaders subsequent and in recent times,' Beazley says, 'and there's been obsession in their offices that they should control the entire messaging from the government. That nobody goes out there to make a presentation of any sort on policy but that it's ticked off at the prime ministerial office level. That's the antithesis of good government. Bob sat all the new ministers down one by one, and he said, "You know the party policy in your area. You know what needs to be done to turn that policy into an implementable government activity. I will intervene in one of two circumstances: one, you ask me to, you want my help with something; two, if something that you're doing crosses with somebody else's portfolio, I'll resolve the dispute."

'He actually understood that his reputation would be built on the backs of strong effective ministers of good public reputation. He, of all the leaders I've seen in my time in politics, is almost unique in his belief that he shone brighter when other people shone with him.'

What about his famous withering put-downs within cabinet? Was Beazley ever at the end of one of his grenades?

'No, but he could go off his trolley with annoyance at some-body. Barry Jones was a marvellous man and a good science minister, but he had real trouble translating it into policy. He had made one of his umpteenth speeches about the significance of science to the cabinet but he wasn't in the cabinet meeting when a science matter was before the cabinet. Bob said, "Barry, where's the *fucking* policy?!" He could be pretty rough in the put-down but it was so rare.'

Was Hawke a good master to serve?

'[Hawke was] our best peacetime prime minister. Nobody who succeeded him is that good and nobody who preceded him was that good. Others have served longer but not as com-prehensively, ably and purposefully as he did. Or with as much confidence. In all the elections since he ceased to be prime minister, there is no more popular figure in demand by Labor Party candidates and Labor Party campaigns in all the states of the Commonwealth, in all the constituencies.'

Still, Hawke's prime ministership ended in blood, not glory. And according to Beazley's biographer Peter FitzSimons, Beazley 'was absolutely gutted by the fight between Hawke and Keating. The last man left standing at Hawke's left elbow was Kim Christian Beazley, despite extraordinary pressure that had been brought to bear for him to crumple and fold and walk away from Hawke.'

Says Hawke: 'This was a very, very tough time for him, because he respected Paul enormously. He has said on occasion to me that, in a sense, part of the spark of political life went out for him after that struggle.'

Almost a quarter of a century after the December 1991 coup, Beazley says it became the turning point in his own political career; a darkening of the spirit that had propelled him into public office.

'Politics till that point of time had been a real source of joy, a real sense of achievement,' he says. 'From that point on it became a grind. You did it not so much from what pleasure you were taking out of it, but you just made the clear determination of what you actually wanted for your country and you just got on with it. Maybe it was just me getting older. All of a sudden it looks to be more of your life behind you than is ahead of you. Maybe it was just the sobriety that came with that perception. I was sad for a long time.'

Sad or not, Beazley, who served as deputy prime minister in the Keating government, says he has 'a great affection' for his mentor's saboteur.

'Paul was a genius who emerged from a totally different background, in many ways a more ordinary Australian one, to Bob. He was the classic self-educated man and an immensely cultured person. He has a very different character to Bob. Bob is very open. He lives out there, he lives a massive life. Paul is very private. Lives a closed life. He lets little pieces of him be exposed to the public. He does get expansive on one or two subjects that fascinate him. A lady was telling me the other day, she was just wandering around the new development at Barangaroo, around Sydney Harbour. Paul happened to be walking along with his grandchildren and she says, "Hello, Mr Prime Minister, really good to see you . . . we're really interested in what you've done down here." Paul then took her on a half-hour tour of the new developments.

'Paul's very generous-hearted, he is,' says Beazley. 'He wouldn't go looking out of his way to communicate in that fashion, but once in a situation where the approach has been made, then yeah, he will respond with generosity and heart. Hawke, quintessentially the public man living in the glaring daylight. Paul, quintessentially the private man picking his moments.'

How do you respond, then, as a friend and admirer of both, when Keating talks about Hawke sleepwalking as prime minister after 1984? And when he posits that it was he, and not Hawke, who was responsible for the grand reforms that characterised the government?

'It's bull-crap,' says Beazley.

Bull-crap?

'Yeah. It's just so – it's such a million miles from the truth. Now that's not to say . . . I don't in any way belittle Paul's contribution, it was substantial. [But] Paul tends to forget quite a bit.

'I think Paul actually had the view that there wasn't much left of him when he became prime minister . . . that he gave all that energy to Bob in his mind. There's enough credit to go around for what was Australia's greatest peacetime government. You don't have to try and chase it all for yourself.'

Hawke is different, says Beazley.

'Bob doesn't go around talking like that about anyone who was in cabinet with him because he was not there in his mind competing with them for the limelight. The limelight came automatically to them and he's prepared to trust his reputation to history.'

In his final speech to the House, Hawke said he 'had no hesitation in declaring his love' for you, I remind Beazley.

'Well, I love him, too,' says Beazley. 'In fact, you are making me feel completely bloody miserable, because this is the first time I've been in Sydney in recent times when I haven't dropped in to see him. I hear he's poorly.'

If Hawke handled his shafting by Keating well, how does he take ageing?

'He hates it. It's so unfair,' says Beazley. 'Bob in spirit is the man forever young, forever interested, forever engaged, forever fascinated with his surroundings.'

— CHAPTER 9 —

ON BEING
A POLITICIAN

I T'S THE END OF JULY 2016, AND THE AMERICAN ELECTION is closing in on its final trimester. I decide to quiz Hawke on what character traits it takes to be a country's leader (according to his former foreign minister Gareth Evans, these include 'levels of insensitivity unknown to ordinary mortals' and a 'deeply flawed personality'), as well as his opinion on the current state of the ALP and significant leaders of the nineteenth and twentieth centuries.

So let's bring the curious reader into the sunken living room of the Right Honourable Robert Lee Hawke, whom we see supine beneath a man of Charles Atlas dimensions, the aforementioned Ryan Barraclough, with what appears to be a baby seal made of foam under their combined weight.

It's the Oov, mentioned earlier, which is doing its 'stimulation of intervertebral disc lubrication' thing.

If the sudokus and cryptic crosswords keep the mind supple, the weekly manipulations by his trainer keep Hawke limber and strong. After being rocked back and forth for a few more minutes, he disappears briefly, then returns, eyes wide with expectation.

'Got a cigar?'

While the lighting ritual unfolds – the snapping of the end, the failed lighter, the uncooperative matches refusing to ignite in the stiff northerly wind – we discuss the Democratic convention in the US.

Been watching it? I ask.

'Aye, a bit. It's a funny bloody country, isn't it?' says Hawke.

What did you think of Bill Clinton's speech about Hillary, where he spoke about their great love affair?

'And with other people?' Hawke laughs. The cigar booms into life like an old car kicked alive. He nods; I can begin.

What are the basic qualities a prime minister must have, and what qualities do you feel you have?

'You must be able to relate to people,' says Hawke. 'One of the paradoxes of politicians is that they represent people, but so many of them are frightened of people. I've been amazed when I've gone around with all of my colleagues and just seen how basically uncomfortable they are. I've always loved the Australian people. I feel at ease with them and, maybe naturally, they've reciprocated. I think that's probably the number-one requirement.'

Other requirements?

'You need to have a capacity for hard work. The hours are horrendous. They've got to be. You've got to be a good listener. People think of politicians as talkers, but a good politician is a good listener. A fair degree of intelligence helps.'

Were there any moments when you had to compromise your ideals for the greater good?

'You've got to be prepared to compromise. You can't always get exactly your own way,' says Hawke. 'My cabinet, universally regarded as probably the best cabinet since Federation, made a rule at the beginning. I didn't impose it. Most of our decisions were by consensus, but they had a rule that if the prime minister was in a minority, the prime minister's decision prevailed. An outstanding example of that was the Antarctic.'

Of his eight years in the chair, Hawke references two decisions as his bravest and most significant: to attack apartheid using financial sanctions, and buddying up with Jacques Cousteau and French prime minister Michel Rocard to protect 14 million square kilometres of the world's last great wildernesses, Antarctica, from mining.

'I was reading cabinet papers over the weekend and this bloody submission was there from the attorney-general [Gareth Evans] and from the Minister for the Environment [Graham Richardson] to endorse CRAMRA, which was the Convention for the Regulation of Antarctic Mineral Resources,' he says.

Richo backed it because he figured some sort of regulation was better than nothing. And Evans felt it would it be too damaging to international relations not to sign a convention that had taken six years to prepare, with negotiations led principally by Australia, and was backed by heavyweight sluggers, the US and Britain.

Hawke and, notably, Keating recoiled.

'I just said, "No bloody way!" I met with the cabinet but they said, "There's nothing we can do, Prime Minister. You'll be working on this for years." I said, "Bugger that. That's it." I went straight off to France and got stuck into it.'

It took eighteen months of intense lobbying, but by 1991, Hawke and Rocard had created the Madrid Protocol that nailed Antarctica shut to drills for fifty years.

The Australian director of international polar conservation organisation Le Cercle Polaire, Neil Hamilton, describes it as 'the most important international environmental agreement ever signed'.

Hawke says, 'When we pulled it off, Gareth said, "You old bugger. You were right." I said, "Yes, I was, Gareth."'

Evans concedes he was 'sceptical at the beginning because I thought it was inconsistent with our international treaty obligations and it was probably unsellable and deliverable. I wasn't objecting to the concept of locking the place up from mineral exploration . . . He proved me wrong because that was one of the significant achievements of the government. He was right and his instinct was pretty good on a lot of that foreign policy stuff.'

Decisions didn't always go Hawke's way, though.

When he went in to bat for the Jawoyn people, who objected to mining on their traditional lands in and around Coronation Hill in Kakadu National Park, for fear it would disturb the creation being Bula, he pushed it so hard within cabinet he reckons it cost him his job.

'I really castigated the cabinet. I'd never spoken to them as harshly, severely and critically at any point before,' says Hawke. 'A lot of my cabinet said we can't stop development because of a bloody underground serpent.'

Hawke threw their own beliefs against them.

'I just said, "The hypocrisy of you people astounds me. You don't have any trouble accommodating to the beliefs of the Holy Trinity, the Resurrection. You easily accommodate that, but the beliefs of other people you treat with contempt."'

The leader of the opposition, Dr John Hewson, claimed, 'If you know anything about Aboriginal heritage, Bula didn't exist ten years ago. He suddenly emerged as a device to block Coronation Hill.'

The Australian Mining Industry Council came out swinging, running full-page advertisements which read, 'Can we afford to let Mr Hawke make a $38 billion mistake?'

Hawke's fury was evident in his cabinet speech:

This supercilious, supremacist discrimination is abhorrent to everything I hold most important and to what in the end I

believe the party stands for . . . We would never contemplate repudiating such findings if they were in respect of the white community and its beliefs. But three hundred blacks are different. You don't want to say it really, but *they* are talking bullshit. We won't say so, but if we give the miners another twelve months to put the pressure on them, the poor silly buggers might come to their senses and think like us! Or at least like Hewson and the miners. Well, as far as I'm concerned, I don't want any part of that hypocrisy and I don't want any part of that discrimination.

On that one, Evans says, 'Hawkey was just getting a bit carried away with the romance of it. There was a bit of the sense that he was losing the plot of it in terms of getting his balances right.'

Hawke tells me, 'These were a *terribly* unjustly treated people. Great gaps in education, health and life expectancy. It was intolerable. I just believed that we had to do everything we could to improve their lot in life.'

Given the rule that the prime minister's decision prevailed, even if it was a minority view, Hawke carried the day. And later that year Keating, whose supporters secured extra votes with a pledge that the decision would be reversed, became prime minister.

The Madrid Protocol. Coronation Hill. Where does your environmentalism come from? I ask.

'I just believed we had an obligation to future generations to preserve for them the wonderful environment with which they'd have been blessed. That we had an obligation to future generations to do all we could in regard to issues concerning environment.'

What are the great joys of being prime minister?

'The fact that every day you can do something that's going to help some people or a lot of people. You're given an *enormous* opportunity there to make your country and the world a better place. And it's an enormous honour, responsibility and opportunity. I woke up every morning looking forward to the day. It was just a totally consuming job.'

What are the lowest points of the job?

Hawke names 1984 as the nadir; 'a terribly low point for me. I went through that campaign in physical *agony*, just *physical agony*.'

Shortly after calling an early election, Hawke was batting for the Prime Minister's XI in its traditional match against the Canberra press gallery. He missed an easy hook shot and copped the ball in his face. His spectacles were smashed, filling his right eye with shards of glass.

What sort of journalist bounces a prime minister?!

'It was a terrible case of batting, because it was a very ordinary delivery and I should've hit the fucking thing for six,' says Hawke, who had his revenge while on the hustings at a naval base in Nowra later in the year.

Surrounded by press, he was asked by the naval commander if he'd like to ride in the little transport basket suspended between two ships.

'Not me, but I've got someone who will,' said Hawke, pointing at journalist Gary O'Neill.

Not long before, Hawke found out that his youngest daughter Rosslyn, who was twenty-four and had just given birth to her second child, was a heroin addict. She weighed thirty-eight kilograms and was expected to die if she continued to use.

'I was devastated and overwhelmed by sorrow for this beautiful girl, who as a youngster had always been able to get me to spoil her, but with whom I had spent too little time when she became a teenager,' remembers Hawke. 'That was without any doubt the lowest period of my time in office. I was just distraught, but I had to get on and I did.'

What do you consider the worst position in which you were ever placed as prime minister?

'One of the hardest things I had to do was to sack Mick Young. He was a very close mate and we had the Combe–Ivanov affair come up. We'd had a secret cabinet meeting on it. Mick went and talked about it to Walshy [Eric Walsh], a journalist mate of his, and I had no alternative but to sack him.'

The Combe–Ivanov affair was a spy scandal thrown at the government a few weeks after taking office. The former ALP national secretary turned political lobbyist David Combe was accused by ASIO of compromising national security by buddying up with Soviet diplomat, and former KGB officer, Valery Ivanov.

Hawke responded by expelling Ivanov.

'If you kick him it out it will damage Australian–Soviet relations,' said Harvey Barnett, the director-general of ASIO.

'Fuck the Russians,' snapped Hawke.

Combe's access to the government was cut off. As a former Labor man whose bread and butter as a lobbyist lay in his access and friendship with government ministers, it was a sharp, if necessary, blow.

'I was accused of being a bastard who had dumped his mate and behaved cruelly towards him,' writes Hawke.

As hard as it was squeezing out David Combe, sacking Mick cut Hawke deep.

'That was a terribly difficult decision – *terribly,*' he says. 'He, of course, was very hurt.'

How do you sack someone who is a good friend?

'You just have to do it. I said, "Mate, you've got to go."'

How did he take it?

'Not well.'

Hawke pauses, thinks.

'But if I'd prevaricated on that, on a question of national

security, it would have put our government in jeopardy. There was just no doubt what had to be done.'

I tell Hawke I want to run through of couple of Machiavelli's principles of leadership, given the brutality of politics.

Try to avoid being hated, except during times of war.

'The issue never arose with me. I always tried to bring the people with me, right from the very, very beginning. That was my approach.'

A leader must act with cunning, and if necessary, force.

'I don't like the word cunning,' says Hawke. 'It has unsavoury overtones. There are times when you've got to play your cards carefully. You won't necessarily disclose everything at the beginning. Gradually try to get people to a point of view. You have to act cleverly.'

People will inevitably lie to you, so it is therefore acceptable for you to lie to them.

'No. I don't accept that proposition at all.'

Trust no one.

'I don't accept that.'

A prince would only be successful when he utilised the strength of his ministers. Collaboration created comradery and no room for disunity and rebellion.

'I agree absolutely with that. My cabinet responded marvellously to my leadership. We strove for, and nearly always got, consensus. If there wasn't, as I said, my view prevailed. They were not unhappy about that. It was their decision.'

I suggest to Hawke his might be the last cabinet where ministers were household names – for the right reasons.

'Before John Hewson went into parliament he was a journalist and he wrote that it was the best cabinet since Federation.

I haven't heard anyone disagree with that. There certainly hasn't been one since to match it.'

Hawke leans forward, rests his cigar on an ashtray.

'It's a marvellous comment on the Labor Party. All the funny and not-so-pleasant Machiavellian stuff that goes on, all the factional fires going on – in some mysterious, magical way, out of all that came this marvellous collection of people.'

Was it a fluke, this confluence of talent?

'I don't know,' says Hawke. 'I'm very grateful, whatever it was.'

Another principle of Machiavelli: *Read history and reflect upon the deeds of outstanding men.* Would you agree?

'Yes, very much so. You're a fool if you can't learn from others. In the end, it's not a question of aping others – you've got to be your own man – but, as I say, you're a fool if you don't try and learn.'

Do you believe nations have seasonal variations? A summer, a spring, an autumn, a winter? And how would you describe the Hawke government?

'Ours was a spring, if you like,' says Hawke.

He references the statement by Singapore's founding prime minister Lee Kuan Yew, who said in 1980 that if Australia kept going the way it was, 'it'll finish up the poor white trash of Asia.'

'There was a lot of truth in that,' Hawke concedes. 'We came through the war in good shape compared to Europe. There was an enormous demand and high prices for our primary products and then for our mineral products. We had an easy run. Then you had the oil crisis in the seventies. The lucky country soon would come to an end. When I was elected, we had double-digit unemployment and double-digit inflation. This was a frightful situation. Fundamental changes had to be made. That's why we had the economic summit when we came into office. Tell the people, let them know the enormity of the situation we face.'

What kind of leader was Lee Kuan Yew?

'Highly intelligent. Justifiably arrogant. He was a very tough leader. People were very critical of the tough regime he had there, but people had forgotten that the communist threat was very real. Infiltrating, coming down through Asia. He was determined that they were not going to get control of Singapore. He had a very tough regime, but he was justified in what he did.'

Do you think politicians are unfairly criticised?

'Yeah, it's become a popular game to sneer at and denigrate politicians. Some of it's their own fault, of course. It's a pity that we're not getting the calibre of people into our parliaments that we should get. This is a problem particularly for the conservative side of politics. On our side, it's more ideologically driven. You look at a businessman, successful businessman. He thinks about politics and he looks at the increasing intrusiveness of the media into his private life, not only of himself, but his family. I think a lot of them are saying, "Bugger it. It's not worth it."'

How would you describe the current state of the Labor Party?

'Still suffering from the awful period we went through, swapping leaders. Rudd. Julia. That was a bad period,' says Hawke.

How does the ALP of 2016 differ from the party you led to four election victories?

'It hasn't got the depth of quality, the people that I was fortunate enough to be blessed with. That's the big difference.'

Who among the current Labor MPs would you welcome into a Hawke cabinet?

'There's none that would replace any of my cabinet.'

Were you euphoric when Kevin Rudd won in 2007?

'I don't want to go into my views about Kevin. It was a Labor victory, and of course I was euphoric.'

Why don't you like talking about Kevin Rudd?

'Simply because I'd have to say things that he wouldn't find pleasing. I don't want to hurt the man.'

Was it the right decision to bring Rudd back in to try to save a few seats at the 2013 election?

'It's not one I would have made.'

Are you kept in the loop by the party when these sorts of big shifts are happening – leadership challenges and so forth?

'Yeah. They still talk to me. Bill [Shorten] was very good to me during his [2016] campaign. He talked to me quite a bit. Asked me if I'd do the advertisement [on Medicare]. I loved getting a taste of that again.'

How do you believe history will record Julia Gillard's prime ministership?

'History will be relatively kind to Julia. She governed under the most extraordinarily difficult circumstances. A minority government, and internal problems with Kevin, others. She did some good things in education, the environment.'

How does it feel, as a sitting PM, to be rolled by your own party?

'It was hurtful. Of course it was hurtful. As I've said publicly on many occasions since, and I repeat it now, I'm eternally grateful that it happened. If it hadn't, I wouldn't have been able to marry Blanche. We just celebrated our twenty-first wedding anniversary a week ago.'

Well, congratulations.

'We've had the most marvellous time together,' says Hawke dreamily. 'I wouldn't have been able to have that if it hadn't happened. Thank you, Paul.'

Did it take you long to get over it?

'No. I don't live in the past.'

What part did the desire for fame play in your decisions?

'I can honestly say I wasn't seeking fame,' Hawke replies. 'I'm not saying that I didn't enjoy it. I did. It would just be a straight-out lie if I said anything else. But it wasn't a driving thing with me. I just had the feeling of satisfaction that at each stage of the career I was able to help people. Within my student life, I was president of the Guild of Undergraduates at the University of Western Australia. I was a student leader and I achieved considerable reforms there. The ACTU is obvious. As advocate I was responsible for some very significant decisions which lifted the standard and quality of life of all Australians. Then, as president, I was able to also do some important things – not least of which is one that is probably forgotten now, but it was terribly important, and that was the issue of retail price maintenance. Australian manufacturers would not supply retailers with their products unless they agreed to sell them at a fixed price. This was costing Australians billions of dollars. I said to the [McMahon] government, "This is just ridiculous. You're demanding that unions go through a price-fixing process for the tribunals, yet you allow this to go on at great cost to the country." And they wouldn't do anything about it.'

In a bold bid to smash retail price maintenance, the ACTU partnered with the Melbourne discounter Lionel Revelman in establishing a retail store. For the ACTU it was also a chance to open up a significant income stream.

Hawke threatened companies with union boycotts if they didn't supply Bourkes–ACTU. In response, Prime Minister Billy McMahon accused Hawke of 'lawlessness'. Eventually, says Hawke, 'we abolished retail price maintenance and we saved the country literally *billions* of dollars.'

How important is your legacy?

'I don't think about it. The first thing to say is I'm very proud. I don't apologise in any way for being proud, because it's a good record. My mind goes back to my parents. I owe everything to them.'

I ask Hawke to give me his opinion of significant leaders of the previous 150 years. First, the British-born African imperialist Cecil Rhodes, whose legacy scholarship got Hawke to Oxford. Earlier in the year, the hashtag *#rhodesmustfall* had been doing the rounds as black and ethnic students led a campaign to remove the statue of Rhodes at Oxford, labelling him a 'racist mass murderer of Africans'.

'By our standards today, he was not a good man. He exploited African natives to make a fortune,' says Hawke. 'Against that, the legacy left with the scholarships is a lasting benefit. I'm indebted to it. The most recent thing about tearing down his statue I think was just silly. You can't go back a century or more and expect the people then should be acting according to the values you've established today.'

Menzies?

'First thing you've got to remember was he got thrown out by his own party at the beginning of the war. Then his government got thrown out because they were incompetent. He didn't come out of that well at all. He inherited a strong economy when he got in in '49. The economy basically looked after itself because, as I said before, the world was paying everything for our products. His anti-communist referendum was just frightful. You've got to give him credit for lasting as long as he did. Of course, he had it on a plate because of the split in the Labor Party. It was a very long period in office. Got to give him credit for that.'

Twenty-three years at the wheel ain't bad.

'He took advantage of the circumstances,' says Hawke.

John F. Kennedy?

'He was a very considerable figure. A charismatic bloke. He wasn't a bad president.'

JFK's brother Robert?

'He's a different character. I was no fan of Robert Kennedy. I don't think he had outstanding values. He ... uh ... the poor bugger, he got shot, too. I don't rate him highly.'

What about Harold Holt?

'A very ordinary prime minister. Say this to his credit: he embraced the immigration program that Labor had introduced. I respect that. Very sad demise.'

John Gorton?

'Arrogant.'

Malcolm Fraser?

'The one thing I always say about Malcolm, whenever it comes up with people who denigrate him, I say, "You remember this: he had an impeccable record on issues of race. He was *absolutely outstanding* on that. He should always be remembered with the utmost respect for that.'

Where do you think he got his empathy for minorities?

'Well,' says Hawke, 'people ask me that and I've thought about it. And this may be the explanation: he came from a very privileged, wealthy background. His early education was at home and then he went to Melbourne Grammar. Then he went straight from Melbourne Grammar to Oxford. And I reckon he was probably *very lonely* at Oxford and he probably palled up with a lot of coloured students. I think that was the beginning of it.'

As a prime minister, however, 'he was hopeless. His handling of the economy was hopeless.'

Margaret Thatcher?

'Margaret and I had a love/hate relationship. You know, I was the leader within the Commonwealth Heads of Government that led the fight against apartheid and Margaret was supporting the South African government, so we used to have terrible bloody fights.'

Even so, when Hawke visited London in 1987 only a couple of months after one of their great fights, 'she couldn't have done more to make our visit successful. She instructed every minister to clear their schedules and make time for us. She was not small-minded.'

Do you regard Thatcher as a great leader?

'Yeah, but . . .'

A laugh. Is it absurd for union man Hawke to remember, positively, the Tory prime minister?

'I disagreed with so much of what she stood for and did, particularly her anti-union tactics. But she was, according to her beliefs, an outstanding leader.'

What was curious about Thatcher, Hawke remembers, was the level of antipathy she felt for Germans.

'I always remember when we were at Gallipoli, we were sitting down having a talk, the two of us, and I was amazed at the *hatred* she had for the Germans. Oh, it was *visceral*.'

Bill Clinton?

'Generally speaking he was a good president.'

Hillary?

'She's a very cold person. I think she's very capable. She'll make a good president.'

The declaration is prophetic. But not in the way Hawke thinks.

— CHAPTER 10 —
SINGO

'**F**UCK ME DRUNK!' SAYS THE MULTI-MULTIMILLIONAIRE John Desmond Singleton, Hawke's pal for close on forty years, telephone pressed against his ear. 'Hawke's changed his fucking number.'

Singo receives me in his penthouse eyrie. Dianna, his secretary of thirty years, leads me into a wood-panelled office outfitted with two gifts from rugby league identity Jack Gibson (the little eight-bar xylophone used until 1970 to announce the news and Jack's old desk microphone), a vintage typewriter that was Singo's copywriting tool until relatively recently, oil paintings by Arthur Boyd (*Parrots* and *Figure Near the Homestead*) and Barry Humphries (*John Olsen in the Flinders*) and a formidable desk wider than a big man's arm.

For a man of seventy-five who's seen it all and done it all – six wives, seven kids, connected to every significant business and political leader over five decades, owner of pubs, horses and radio stations – Singo looks strong, fresh.

A little surprised by his rude health, I'm reminded of the stoush he had with his pal Hungry Jack's founder Jack Cowin at a

Sydney waterfront restaurant in 2015. Depending on your interpretation of the paparazzi photos, Singo was either about to slice off Cowin's ear with a broken bottle or engaging in an awesomely authentic piece of street theatre. I saw the photos and laughed. How could a man of such vintage be considered threatening?

Then I meet him.

Even in the winter of his life (he's the oldest Singleton ever, which 'fucking gives you pause for reflection, mate,' he says), he's still a good six foot in the sneakers he pairs with R.M. Williams moleskins and a flawlessly pressed button-up shirt, a corduroy jacket draped over his high-backed chair. Singo's hair is cut close to the scalp, grey but not white, and the cartoon features – the Joker smile, Bugs Bunny teeth and golf ball cheeks – combine to create a compelling and, yeah, attractive face.

It isn't a stretch to call Singo a national treasure. In a country where 'true blue' has atrophied into a nasty little racist stereotype, Singo is the take-no-shit, tell-it-like-it-is-and-don't-cry-about-the-consequences Aussie. Rafferty. Hogan. McKenzie. Singleton. Hawke. When Singo dies – which he eventually will, despite his aura of immortality – a part of the Australian character will disappear with him.

It's why he liked Hawke and it's why their friendship flourished, despite their cavernous political differences. As he'll tell me later in the interview, 'Somehow or other, mate, we built a relationship without ever saying it to one another. He just became a mate and I felt that even though we were on so-called different sides, we were on the same side. We were on the Australian side. We just had different ways of scoring a try.'

When I enter, Singo is examining his phone. It takes a little to convince him that the book I'm writing on Hawke is authorised and, twenty minutes later, as if to flush me out as an imposter, he pulls out the phone again, eyeballs me and says, 'I'm ringing him up.'

Of course, Mr Singleton.

'I'm just going to ring him to ask him if there's anything he doesn't want me to say. See how long he's on the phone for.'

After punching in the wrong numbers ('fuck me drunk' etc.), Singo works out the right sequence and the call lands.

Hawke's secretary: 'Good afternoon, Mr Hawke's office.'

In comic politesse, vowels drawn out in Menzies-esque exaggerated tones: 'Good aaaafternoon, it's John Singleton for the prime minister, please.'

Hawke's secretary: 'Hello, he's actually in Melbourne at the moment. He'll be back tomorrow afternoon. Can I get him to call you?'

John Singleton: 'Yes, tomorrow afternoon will be fine. You shouldn't let him travel so often.'

Hawke's secretary: 'He's very stubborn.'

John Singleton: 'Stubborn? Really? You surprise me. Alright, darling, I won't trouble him down there. Get him to call me though, love. Thanks, love.'

Singo looks back at me, and my confidence seems to convince him. I tell him I want to hear the story of Hawke moving into Singo's harbourfront palace when he got rolled by Keating in 1991.

Labor senator and member of the socialist left John Faulkner ('One of the brightest guys I've met in my life in politics . . . a genius . . . could've been prime minister,' says Singo) had met Singo at Aussies Café in Parliament House in December 1991 and told him Hawke was about to be challenged by Keating for a second time – and this time he was going to lose. Could Singleton tell his old pal the news, maybe convince him not to challenge?

'Why would you want me to tell him?' asked Singo.

'Because you're the only one he'll listen to,' said Faulkner.

Singo made the call.

'So I said to Hawkey, "Look, I need to see ya . . . [it's] personal."'

'What about?' said Hawke, who was busy studying the form guide (race five, Rosehill).

'I said, "Mate, there's going to be another bloody move to replace you and you're gonna lose. And that comes from John Faulkner."'

'"Why did he get you to tell me?"'

'"Good fucking question. Why don't you ask him?"'

'"I'm not talking to that cunt."'

'I said, "Well he probably feels the same. That's probably why I'm the middleman here. I don't like it."'

'Oh . . . fucking . . . he'll never beat me, he'll never . . .'

'Well, you're probably right, you've never been beaten. Okay, I've passed on the message.'

That afternoon, as Singo was on his way home from Canberra, he realised – and he can't remember the exact circumstances of the realisation; maybe he called Faulkner, maybe Faulkner called him – that if he was any good as a mate, he'd help Hawke make the next step, the transition from being most important man in the country to unemployed sixty-two-year-old senior citizen.

Singo called Hawke again.

'I said to him, "Mate, you hate hypotheticals, I know that's a good way to dodge questions on TV, but here's a real question . . . I have double-checked and I too believe you're going to get rolled. Listen, just say you get beaten. Faulkner's a cunt, we all know that. All the left's a cunt. Keating's a cunt, we all know that. But say he does win? You get thrown out of the Lodge. You're not going to get beat, but other prime ministers, when they have got beat, how long do they have to get out of the Lodge? Do they go and live in a Holiday Inn? What do they fucking do? They have a plan B. You are going to get beat and the day after you get beat I happen to be going to America for six weeks. You'll have nowhere to go, and you've been to my joint...'

Here, Singo digresses into an oral tour of the house: 'You could drive into my joint, straight into the bedrooms upstairs, living room, and downstairs with a pool. Waterfront, wharf, boat, a Scarab [gaudy eighties cigarette speedboat]. Plenty of space for Bob to sunbake'.

'I said, "Mate, you can stay at my joint for six weeks."'... Sure enough, the next day he was out of a job, nowhere to live. And he moved in.'

How was Hawke's state of mind post-defeat?

'Mate, unlike Paul, instantly on to what's next. He learned a lot there. He learned how to buy milk and everything. You give them money, they give you milk.'

Singo compares Hawke's response favourably to John Howard's dignified 'the things that unite us are more important than the things that divide us' speech, after being brought down in the election of 2007, including the ignominy of losing his own seat.

'No quivering of the bottom lip like that wuss Fraser. No self-important speeches like with Gough and these other cunts. Fucking cop it on the chin and move on.'

Four years earlier, Hawke had cemented their friendship when he employed John Singleton Advertising to run the Labor Party election campaign, a switcheroo for a gun who'd created anti-Labor ads in 1974 and who was the driving force behind the ferociously right-wing Workers' Party.

But Hawke, who'd kept the bulk of the bureaucrats who served Fraser when he won office in 1983, was never one for cheap payback. He instinctively knew a good leader checks his spite at the door. Hawke wanted excellence at every tier of government if he was going to govern well and convince the electorate that Labor, and not the conservatives, was the natural party of government. And by the time of the 1987 election – Hawke's third as leader – when Labor was sliding in the polls, Hawke wanted the best, even if it meant consorting with the enemy.

At a black-tie dinner party, Hawke tugged Singo by the sleeve of his dinner jacket.

'Unbelievable! Imagine this happening,' says Singo. 'He said, "Listen, mate, these polls, all the advertising, all the advice in there is all shit." He said, "You're the only one that knows this business, and I've got a deal for you. If I get you to handle the campaign, with all the differences we have philosophically, you have to be on my side. You have to sell my point of view and you have to promise never to dud me . . . ever." I said, "Mate, I'd love to. I agree with everything you say, mate. You're a genius, I'm a mug, but I will never ever dud ya." And we shook hands, we went on with the dinner party.'

Hawke, says Singo, had come to realise 'that I was at least straight arrow. I wasn't going to bullshit I agreed with all their policies. As if, you know? I said, "Mate, I'll bloody get other people to think it's good just as long as you realise I don't. I'm not here to be brainwashed. I'm here to brainwash other people."'

The socialist left were apoplectic.

'The next day he announced to the cabinet that I'd taken over. He had the mass walkout and resignations . . . They were all up in arms. "You can't do this, you can't do that. You never know what he's going to do next." And Hawke said, "He's given me his word, that's it. And if you want to resign, good. Please yourself."'

The campaign was classic Singo. It included the TV spot with the quickly immortalised Whingeing Wendy, an actor playing a suburban housewife. We find Wendy in her kitchen, facing the camera and delivering a monologue to wannabe prime minister John Howard in the broadest Australian accent:

'Mr Howard, me and my family would like to ask you some rool simple questions, like about your free-money-for-nothing promises. Where is your eight-billion-dollar tax cut money roolly coming from? Will you cut home nursing? Will you cut out two million Meals on Wheels?'

Coupled with the feel-good jingle, 'Let's Stick Together', 'We clawed back, we jumped back, raced back,' says Singo. 'I remember down at the Hyatt in Melbourne the night when the results were there. I was sitting in a room with Clem, Bob's dad . . . Then the early polls come through from Vaucluse – box one or something ridiculous – and John Elliot . . . declared John [Howard] the new prime minister . . . And I'm just with Bob's dad, who's teary deary. He's old, and he's pretty emotional about his son getting flogged. I'm saying whatever reassuring words I can come up with at the time: "Don't believe everything you read on the TV." Then Hawkey comes and I say, "Hey, you better come sit with your dad. He's pretty upset."'

'"Ah, that's a lot of bullshit!" says Hawke.

'Him and Richo, mate, they could read the polls. They would know hours before the media. Between Richo and Hawkey and [Bob] McMullan, they knew that we were going to shit in and so while the [television stations] were announcing the Liberals, they were quietly celebrating their victory.'

Even when NSW Labor was buried in the 1988 landslide to Nick Greiner's Liberals, Hawke had Singo's back, calling to reassure him it wasn't the fault of his agency.

'He said, "Just want you to know that was a fuck-up, that campaign, and it wasn't your fuck-up. We're working together as long as I'm prime minister, right?"

'"Right."

'"So get that sad look off your face."

'I said, "I haven't got a sad look on my face."

'"Bullshit! You will have. You'll be blaming yourself. Not your fault. Let's get set down and stuck into this fucking Peacock now. I'm going to carve him up."

'That was a nice thing, he didn't have to do that,' says Singo. 'Mate, he's just been a treasure.'

Tell me about women around Hawke.

'Wandering around with him before and after he was prime minister, he's like the Beatles. They want to touch him, have a piece of him. He was a freak show. Walked into a public bar at El Rancho at Epping one night when his driver was Graham Richardson, the later Minister for Health. A hanger-onerer was Bill Hayden, later governor-general. We were having a few schooners after a TV show and the birds all came from every-where. This is a trade union leader. He had a charisma that was unbelievable, mate.'

Can you explain that effect he had on women?

'No I can't, because I often thought about it. There I am and they're all crowding around him. I was young, long blond hair. He had that bloody hair of his and that terrible ocker voice, more than I did. They were all going for him . . . I was just picking up the scraps.'

And his ability to drink? Is the reputation warranted?

'He drank like a twenty-stone bloke,' says Singo. 'A glass of beer was a glass of beer – you drink it then you have another one. I'm a fast drinker, but not in his class. He was world-class. But he would never become maudlin or reflective, as if he'd disciplined himself to become more intellectual. His embrace of general knowledge, world knowledge, currency exchanges, trade – and then straight on to the fifth at Canterbury. With equal enthusiasm. He's only ever been touched on the other side of politics by Alan Jones. Totally different person, abso-lutely nothing in common, except they both know everything about everything. Mate, there'll never be another Hawkey. He was just fabulous.'

Sometimes, says Singo, Hawke'd call him up and talk 'about nothing, because his mind was full of UNESCO and bloody NATO and all that other shit and pretending we had a defence force and having to suck up to America who'd made mistake after mistake. What were we supposed to do? Depend on these submarines now? Never been built, never going to be built. It's always been a joke. So you've got to agree with America, no matter how dopey they are. And he'd just say, "Mate, why don't you come over, we'll just discuss fishing in Persia or something."

'I was someone he knew he could turn to despite our differences. He used to say, "Do you really believe that what we're doing's wrong?" I'd say, "Yeah, because I think this, and this, and this. But if you can't get into office you can't do any fucking thing. At least when you're in office you can do something, so I'd rather be on your side . . ."'

How do you compare Hawke as prime minister to Australia's current leader, the thoroughly honourable Malcolm Turnbull?

'One was the prime minister, the other is a debate about what he's doing there and how long he is going to be there.'

For Hawke's seventieth birthday in 1999, Singo gifted his pal a quarter-share in Belle du Jour, a horse he'd bought on the Gold Coast for $200,000 earlier in the year. The filly would win millions, including a 'freakish' win at the 2000 Golden Slipper.

'I wouldn't have given it to him if I knew how much he was going to fucking make,' says Singo. 'I didn't realise it was his seventieth birthday. If I went to your birthday I'd no more think of buying you a present than fly to the moon. You might take a leg of lamb if you're a butcher or something, or because you're walking past a butcher shop. Or when I owned a brewery, you might say, "Look, I'll supply the keg." But I haven't bought anyone a present – sisters, brothers, fucking friends.'

Uncharacteristically, however, Singo opened his mouth and told Hawke he was now the part-owner in one of his horses. Later in the night, Hawke asked for its name. Singo picked one out of his head. Belle du Jour. Other part-owners included the veterinarian Gerry Rose and his wife Helen.

'And Gerry Rose fucking hates the Labor Party!' booms Singo. 'His wife even more so! I said [to myself], "Well, look, I've already done it, I can't say take another one." Mind you, his opinion was whichever one I gave him would have won. He's that self-confident . . . cunt. Anyway, they [Hawke and the Roses] get on great!'

If one of his horses has a real shot at winning, Singo always places a bet equal to fifth-place prize money. At the Golden Slipper in 2000 it was a hundred grand for fifth. Belle du Jour was ten-to-one to win. That meant a million for a win which, as Singo helpfully points out, is 'a lot of money. Sixteen years ago, even more money.'

Singo told his partners they had around 250 K in winnings to date locked away. Did they want to share the $100,000 bet? 'I don't care. I'm happy with it all,' Singo said. 'But we do have the money in the bank.'

To seal it, he tells 'em, 'By the way, [trainer] Clarry [Conners] said first five for sure, unless something goes wrong. But we do have the money in the bank.'

Gerry says, 'Yeah, I'm in.'

Blanche turns to Bob: 'Well, we didn't have it in the first place – why don't we? Make a day of it, yeah? It's not going to cost anything, it's already in the bank.'

Famously, the horse misses the start. Rears. Almost tosses jockey Lenny Beasley. Belted by nerves, Singo and Bob go to watch the race from the restaurant rather than the owners' room.

Bob says, 'That's not our horse is it?'

'Yeah.'

Bob: 'Can't win from there, can it?'

'No!'

'Hopeless, hopeless, hopeless,' remembers Singo.

And then, on the home straight, as if guided by a divine hand, the pack parts and Belle du Jour rides straight through and wins by a nose.

'Shits it in,' says Singo.

The three men are so aroused by the joy, by the disbelief, by the thought of a million bucks swinging into their joint bank account, 'everyone thought Hawkey was on the piss again. They thought I was absolutely out of my tree on grog,' says Singo. 'It looked like three drunks dragged out of a pub after a race win. It hadn't helped that Gerry Rose had put these hats on us back to front. Someone described it as I looked like a cross between Lleyton Hewitt and Dorian Gray. I had my hair cut short ever since. I used to have long blond hair, but *long* . . . Fuck it looked terrible. Then I shouted the whole pub. But not the members. Fuck the members.'

The public bar is still named Belle du Jour in honour of Singo's hour-long spree.

'It was fucking unbelievable,' says Singo. 'Bob finished up from that horse probably winning one and a half million tax free.'

Does he ever wish he'd bought Bob a tie instead?

'I could have bought the very best tie,' says Singo wistfully, though when I mention that it's Hawke's eighty-seventh birthday in two days' time, and that if Singo could slip him another quarter-share it might reignite their old luck, he smiles.

'I bought a horse called Big Brown which fucked up all my mares. I had twelve very good years and then two bad ones, but I'll have a good year this year. I might do that.'

Whatever happens, the friendship isn't going anywhere.

'I'm not a suck. I've never sucked up to him. I've never sucked up to any cunt, but I said, "I really think, mate, you're doing great. And I like going out with ya in public because I feel like I'm the drummer in the rock band."'

Pointedly, 'I never got a favour off him in my fucking life. I didn't get any fucking thing, you know.'

Except.

'Except a great friendship. Which will do.'

— CHAPTER 11 —

ENDING APARTHEID

T HAT WHOLE THING ABOUT NOT REMEMBERING THE sixties because they were so damn fun?

Everyone remembers the gloomy 1980s.

Interesting sex was a death sentence, jobs didn't exist and the planet teetered on the precipice of catastrophic nuclear war as the dying Soviet Empire bankrupted itself trying to match, ICBM for ICBM, an America emboldened by its hard-line, former-actor president.

At school we practised scrambling under our desks if we heard the siren to indicate an atomic bomb had been dropped. At home, I examined nuclear shelter catalogues I found in my dad's briefcase.

Television forgot, briefly, its obsession with Holocaust porn and turned its lazy eye to end-of-the-world themes.

Much worse was a radio awash in anti-apartheid songs. Peter Gabriel lamented the arrest, torture and death of activist Steve Biko at the hands of South Africa's security services.

Multi-racial ska band The Specials wanted to 'Free Nelson Mandela'!

In New York, a collective of righteous superstars, including Bono, Peter Garrett and Lou Reed, formed Artists United Against Apartheid and released the single 'Sun City', jerking around to an off-beat rhythm and vowing never to play the South African resort of the same name. Such beautiful, pointless sentiments, and as effective as posting a *Free Tibet* sticker on your car and expecting a monumental shift in Chinese foreign policy (Elton John and Queen happily played Sun City). What you'd call virtue-signalling in our current epoch. Hit the Share button on Facebook and watch the Likes climb.

What the world needed, and what it eventually got, was the prime minister of a small Pacific country who was determined to skewer South Africa's rotten regime. A man who'd been drilled in the absolute certainty of the Brotherhood of Man. A leader who would shuck diplomatic niceties and mobilise banks to squash what he describes as an 'absolutely repulsive, unacceptable doctrine'.

Hawke had form on apartheid.

'I was conscious of apartheid very early and hated it,' he says. 'Seeing people discriminated against simply on the basis of their colour and not having the right, full rights of citizens of their nation, was against everything that I learned at my father's knee and that had been imbued in me. Then it became a real issue when the Springbok tour came and I led the fight against it. We mobilised not just the trade unions, but a wide range of people in Australia. We significantly disrupted the tour.'

In 1971, South Africa's Springbok rugby team had banned two non-white players from joining their tour to Australia. ACTU president Hawke responded by saying South Africa should be barred from international sport and foreshadowed union bans should the tour go ahead.

Hawke wrote to the South African prime minister, B.J. Vorster – who as the Minister for Justice had helped bang Mandela away for life in 1964 – requesting a non-discriminatory team be chosen for the Australian tour.

The request was rejected.

Therefore, said Hawke, union action was inevitable.

In Australia, the panic button was punched. Newspapers complained in editorials and front-page stories that the unions, under the spell of their Svengali master, ran the country. How did that sit with Hawke?

'If you allowed yourself to be dictated to by what the press thought it'd be a different country to what you have now,' he says. 'People knew that as far as Hawke was concerned there was no room for compromise.'

Labor shrieked and distanced itself from Hawke and the ACTU.

'They had some concerns,' Hawke concedes.

The McMahon government?

Well...

Hawke coughs. The eyebrows ramp north. He eyeballs me as if to say, *You really need me to articulate anything about Billy McMahon's sorry reign?*

I do.

'The McMahon government was absolutely hopeless,' Hawke obliges. 'They had no concept of the enormity of what apartheid meant. That was why non-government acts were so important. That the world would know that within Australia there was a significant strong feeling of repulsion about this policy. And that we wanted to do what we could to bring the attention of the world to how unacceptable this was.'

Not all the unions followed the ACTU's lead.

In Western Australia the Transport Workers Union fuelled the Springboks' plane and shifted their bags. In Melbourne, two workers stood in front of Hawke and burned their union cards. The government said it would bring in the RAAF if any other branches of the TWU sided with the ACTU. Hawke said the ACTU would ruin South African Airways if it flew the team into Australia.

Public opinion was divided, both sides equally passionate.

Hawke's mother Ellie received a call asking, 'Why didn't you strangle him at birth?'

Another caller told her she'd given birth to a 'monster'.

Packages filled with shit were sent to Hawke's Melbourne home. His kids were teased at school. Hawke's youngest daughter Rosslyn was forced to watch 'while a group of children symbolically killed Hawke by grinding his photographs into a paste'.

'It wasn't pleasant, but nothing was going to divert me,' says Hawke.

Did you speak about it as a family?

'Oh yes. They didn't need persuading. They were completely supportive of me and didn't want me to give in. There was a lot of nastiness even among my own movement, because within the trade unions we had people with racist tendencies. It was my job to lead and show that they were wrong. And that it was not only wrong as far as individuals were concerned but as far as Australia was concerned – that it was a mark against our country if we were, in any way, directly or indirectly, to tolerate that sort of policy. We had an obligation to do everything we could.'

Were you surprised by the depth of feeling on both sides?

'I knew that there was a racist element within Australia. It would be foolish to be surprised by that; there's been enough evidence of it. But that's what the essence of leadership is. You're aware of these things and you've got to set an example and try and persuade people that they're not right.'

On a flight to Europe, bound for Israel for an International Labour Organization conference, a person unknown phoned in a bomb threat to Hawke's plane. The bird turned around and landed back in Perth. After it was cleared to fly and had reached its cruising altitude, the captain left the cockpit to talk to Hawke – specifically, to tell his famous passenger that he was 'less than enthusiastic' about the event and, 'By the way, Mr Hawke, it may interest you to know that I am Rhodesian.'

'He was not too happy,' says Hawke. 'But I made clear what my position was.'

In Queensland, premier Joh Bjelke-Petersen declared a state of emergency. The old crook even brokered a secret deal with police to handle the expected anti-apartheid protests. And if in the heat of the moment they roughed up the protesters? Joh promised that zealous police wouldn't be penalised for any action they took to suppress the protests.

Joh also told Police Union president Ron Edington he'd fix the cops' pay rise – which was currently before the industrial court – and they'd get a superannuation fund.

Outside the South Africans' hotel in Brisbane, 600 police met 400 protesters.

'The police took Joh at his word,' recalls one protester. 'They went apeshit on the slope below the Tower Mill, removing their badges and clobbering anyone within reach. Any respect I had for the QPS went out the window that day. They were a bunch of out-of-control thugs.'

Can you describe the mood in the state at the time? Bjelke-Petersen bussing in hundreds of cops from all over the state. Batons. Horses.

'It was very, very nasty, because Joh represented the very worst of the principles that underlay apartheid,' says Hawke.

Do you feel like you, with the ACTU, changed a lot of people's minds about apartheid?

'I'm *sure* we changed a lot of minds,' says Hawke.

South Africa's cricket team were scheduled to tour later in the year, the summer of '71/'72. The chairman of the Australian

Cricket Board, Don Bradman – a man whose legend would make any Australian weak at the joints – got in contact with Hawke and told him they should have a private meeting. The implication was this wouldn't be a discussion about the rights and wrongs of apartheid so much as a personal request for Hawke to keep the union dogs on a leash.

Hawke flew to Adelaide and cabbed it to the Don's house in Kensington Park. Bradman told Hawke he didn't believe politics should intrude on sport and that the tour should proceed.

'And I said, "That's my point entirely,"' says Hawke. 'It wasn't us; it was this government in South Africa that intruded politics into sport by saying that no non-white person had the right to represent the country.'

How did Bradman react?

'Don thought for a moment and he looked at me and he said, "Bob, I haven't got an answer to that." There *is* no answer. *They* introduced politics into sport, not the other way around.'

Cricket talk between the interviewer and Hawke ensues. Did you ask Bradman for tips on your stance? How to emulate his famous drive?

Soon, we fall down a hole of bawdy cricket jokes involving the English fast bowler Fred Trueman and the racism inherent in British society in the fifties, as well as a couple celebrating the physical superiority of West Indian cricketers.

First, Hawke on Trueman.

'Freddie hated batsmen and he was a racist bastard and he particularly hated black batsmen. And there was this black batsman who went on to get a hundred and fifty. And Freddie was getting madder and madder, and Colin Cowdrey told me Freddie bowled a perfect ball, an out-swinger, and it went straight through Cowdrey's legs and to the boundary for four . . .'

Hawke switches to the voice of Colin Cowdrey, mimicking the well-rounded Oxford accent.

'At the end of the over I went up to Freddie and I said, "Oh, Freddie, at the very least I should've kept my legs together." Freddie gave the immortal answer: "Not thee, lad, thy fookin' mother!"'

In the final of the just-created, one-day-format Gillette Cup, Freddie's Yorkshire team faced Northampton.

'Northampton had more coloured players than any other side,' says Hawke. 'And Yorkshire were batting and it was getting pretty tight and Freddie came in to bat. The field crowded around and Freddie took block and just as the bowler was about to start his run-up, Freddie said, "Hold it, ump! If these black bastards don't piss off I'll appeal against the fookin' light!"'

I ask him if he ever met Trueman.

Hawke hoots. 'I *played* against him!'

What was it like to face the demon himself?

'I was twelfth man that day against Yorkshire,' he says, with what might be sheepishness. 'We took him out that night and got him pissed. He didn't bowl very well the next day.'

Hawke switches to the superb West Indian players of the late 1970s.

'Do you remember Joel Garner?' asks Hawke.

Also known as Big Bird?

'Yeah. This girl, this cricket groupie, used to follow Joel Garner. They were playing a test match at the Sydney Cricket Ground and at the end of the day, the cricketers were coming out and this groupie lady looked up at Mr Garner and said, *Mr Garner, are you built in proportion?*

'And he said . . .' Hawke suddenly animates as the Barbados-born Garner. '*Ma'am, if I was built in proportion I'd be eight foot ten!*'

'The other story,' says Hawke, 'was Garner and his captain. They were walking across the Sydney Harbour Bridge at night and they stopped to have a piss. The captain looks at Joel and says, *Geez, it's cold, isn't it?* And Joel says, *And deep too!*'

You don't hear gags like that anymore, at least not in polite company. And the way Hawke tells a gag, the convincing impersonations, his timing building to an uproarious finale, guarantees unexpected snorts of laughter.

But back to apartheid.

What was the most surprising thing that came out of that Springbok tour?

'Just how divided the Australian people were. A large number of the Australian people were good and decent, rejected the concept, but we had to face the fact that there was a strong element of racism in the country.'

Do you believe Australia is particularly racist or do you think there's an element of racism in every country?

'Every country's got an element of it. We're seeing that now all around the world.'

What do you make of Pauline Hanson's re-emergence?

'I'm disappointed, and particularly in a situation where the Senate is so mixed up. It gives these minor parties considerable political influence. I'm very sad to see her back on the scene.'

How would you react if you were prime minister and you saw her walking through the House?

'I'd be civil to her, but I would not be extending any hand of friendship.'

It's an ironic twist of fate that Hawke was only alive to help squash apartheid because a white South African cricketer, Roy McLean, saved his life twenty years earlier.

It was the summer of '52/'53 and Rhodes Scholar Hawke had six months to kill before he sailed for England. In the uni term he tutored students in economics. During the Christmas break he worked as an assistant to the University of Western Australia's gardener.

'I had this very dignified job of taking round a horse and cart loaded with horse shit and spreading it on the roses,' he says. 'I went back and loaded it up again and then said, "Come on," but the horse wouldn't move, so I got out and went round the front to pull it out and it bolted, and the shaft of the cart ripped open the inside of my right thigh. There was blood pouring out and I collapsed onto the side of the cricket oval. It just happened that the South Africans had arrived and were playing an opening game against the Governor's XI on James Oval. I collapsed on the side of the oval and Roy McLean, marvellous batsman, he raced over to me; he had these strong hands, and he just held my thigh together. Otherwise I would have bled to death.'

Four decades later, when Australia and South Africa resumed official test matches, Hawke was invited to South Africa to speak to a gathering of officials and former cricketers.

'Perhaps some of you would like to do something about Roy McLean for saving my life,' cheeky Hawke said.

To which one Boer responded, 'My bloody oath I would.'

Once you were in government, did it become a great resolve to hit apartheid?

'Yes, it did become a great resolve. From the beginning. And the instrument in my hand, obviously, was the Commonwealth Heads of Government meeting.'

It wasn't a stretch. In 1979 Commonwealth leaders, led by Hawke's predecessor Malcolm Fraser, had eased the white-minority-ruled Republic of Rhodesia into the black-majority-ruled Zimbabwe, even if it was under the hammer of Robert Mugabe.

(A side note. In meetings, Hawke says, Zimbabwe's Mugabe would make the 'right noises' about apartheid, 'but they were meaningless. He had his own form of apartheid in the way he treated white people. It had been an extraordinarily productive country and it just went downhill under him.')

'My first CHOGM was in 1983. That was in India and I was the new boy, but it soon emerged that I was a leader of the push against apartheid,' says Hawke. 'The next meeting was 1985 in the Bahamas, and we set up the Eminent Persons Group. There were [trade] sanctions, we tried sanctions on . . . I said to them in 1987, in Vancouver, "Look, sanctions aren't working. They're too easily avoided."'

Hawke says he told the other leaders that the only way to effect any sort of real change was to hurt the South African government financially. Hawke called the internationally renowned investment banker and economist Jim Wolfensohn, who would later become president of the World Bank.

'I rang Jim and he immediately got on a plane and flew to Vancouver. I introduced my idea and he said, "I think it can work." And I said, "If I provide the top people from my treasury, will you work with them and formally get it going?" He said, "Yes, I'd love to."'

There were concerns for Wolfensohn's safety when you were setting up the financial sanctions, weren't there?

'Yes, but that was a risk he was prepared to take,' says Hawke.

Were those threats real?

'It wasn't unknown for the South African regime to assassinate people.'

A robust opponent of the anti-apartheid measures among the Commonwealth heads was the Conservative British prime minister Margaret Thatcher.

'She didn't like the concept of interfering in the political affairs of another country,' says Hawke.

Hawke's buddy in the White House, Ronald Reagan, wasn't much help either. He vetoed a bill in Congress to impose sanctions on South Africa, writing in his diary, 'It isn't a solution to the problem of apartheid and it will hurt the very blacks we're trying to help.'

Meanwhile, sixteen of Australia's best cricketers signed lucrative deals to tour South Africa in '85/'86 and '86/'87, both 'rebel' tours led by the former Australian skipper Kim Hughes. Hawke called the players 'traitors'.

In 1985, world champion surfer Tom Carroll refused to surf in South Africa's three international surfing events 'until black surfers are allowed on all beaches'. Carroll was sponsored by the South African company Instinct, which he claims threatened him with a lawsuit if he didn't compete.

Hawke heard about the threat, called Carroll and invited him to Canberra, where he told the surfer that if his sponsor went legal he had the weight of the Australian government behind him.

'I was really welcomed by Bob. It was a nice feeling to have that support from him,' says Carroll, who didn't lean either way politically and admits he was initially inclined to distrust any politician courting the youth vote. 'I had some strange responses to my decision. All kinds of people went a bit crazy about it. But he was genuine, very interested, and he asked all these really good questions about the tour and competing and where I'd been and even brought up some results. He read his brief very well.'

When Nelson Mandela came to Australia, Hawke introduced him to Carroll.

'I remember Bob telling him, in his frank way, "Nelson, this was the world champion surfer at the time and he made the decision to boycott the events in South Africa." Gave him the whole story. Mandela turned around to me and said, "Thank you very much, Tom. I needed all the help I could get." Bob facilitated that. It was a lovely moment between the three of us. It gives me goosebumps now.'

At Carroll's retirement dinner in 1995, Hawke would say, 'His beliefs, his principles, were so strong that he put those in front of everything else, and as I recall there has been no example in the history of Australian sport where a champion has been prepared to put principles so manifestly in front of his or her own interests as Tom Carroll did in 1985.'

By the 1989 CHOGM in Kuala Lumpur, it was clear the sanctions were helping to turn the screws. The South African economy was shrinking. The following year, apartheid's last head of state, F.W. de Klerk, released Nelson Mandela after twenty-seven years in prison, also lifting his government's ban on Mandela's African National Congress (ANC).

In 1990, the Investor Responsibility Research Center in Washington estimated sanctions had cost South Africa between US$15 and $27 billion.

In the same year, the South African Minister for Finance, Barend du Plessis said financial sanctions were 'the dagger that finally immobilised apartheid'.

'The whole process was self-reinforcing in a way that trade sanctions never were and never could have been,' said Gareth Evans in his Nelson Mandela Day address in 2012.

Every new financial institution in some part of the world refusing credit, or setting tougher terms, increased the risk for other suppliers still in the field. By 1990 the denial of access to new international capital was dramatically and comprehensively strangling the economy. South Africa could fund internally growth of no more than 2 per cent a year, but it needed to grow at least 4 per cent or more to create jobs for its expanding population and to maintain existing standards of living. If nothing had changed, the country would have exploded.

So Australia was, I believe, a prominent and effective

international voice on the anti-apartheid issue over many years. The sports boycott conceived and led by Australia was psychologically important in creating a sense of isolation and vulnerability, and the financial sanctions – in their fullest application again a significantly Australian initiative – were profoundly practically important in their economic and ultimately endgame political impact.

I ask Hawke for his thoughts on South Africa post-apartheid. A country with one of the most unequal distributions of wealth and employment in the world, with 47 per cent of its citizens living on less than US$43 a month. The burning anti-immigrant sentiment. The hate crimes against foreigners. The farm invasions and torture of whites – seventy attacks in the first few months of 2017 alone, including twenty-five murders. A nation that may not have state-sanctioned racism, thanks to leaders like Hawke, but one that is as riven as ever by disunity, mistrust and fear.

'It's a terrible, terrible disappointment,' says Hawke. 'We had such a giant of a man as their first leader in Mandela . . . It's a tragedy that Mandela wasn't able to ensure better succession.'

Have you ever wept for South Africa, Mr Hawke?

'Internally, I weep, yes. Very much so.'

— CHAPTER 12 —

GARETH EVANS

T HE AUSTRALIAN NATIONAL UNIVERSITY IS SPREAD OVER 348 hectares of low-slung, bush-wrapped buildings in its own corner of the capital. Student or passer-by, you can wander into any number of lectures at a uni rated among the twenty best in the world.

Early for my meeting with the university's chancellor, Gareth Evans, AC – Hawke's first attorney-general and later his Nobel Peace Prize-nominated foreign minister – I just miss the wonderfully obscure 'A Japanese Moment in the Globalisation of Contemporary Chinese Art' but briefly catch a session on John Stuart Mill's 1869 essay 'The Subjection of Women', joining an audience busy swiping smartphones and pecking at laptops.

The nearby chancellery building is illuminated by shafts of soft light, the sun filtered by a phalanx of gum trees. Five Fred Ward chairs and accompanying tables fill the waiting room. (Ward, if you didn't know, is the Australian interior designer responsible for the ANU's sober mid-century style, the use of wood and subtle curves suggesting a university not given to fads or gaudy grandeur.) And perhaps because of Gareth's famous exactness (a secret CIA report from 1988 describes him as 'a brilliant but arrogant and impatient foreign minister'), every moment in the building plays as if by script. I walk through the two sets of automatic doors and am immediately greeted by a uniformed security guard who politely recites my name and the time of my meeting. Without my having to ask, a parking pass is presented.

Before I can lower my body into one of the high-backed Wards, the security guard rushes over to sweep me up to the third floor. Here, I'm deposited into a smaller waiting room, near the office that serves the chancellor two days a week.

The chancellor's secretary appears and plays a captivating little game of *What is this?* with a dagger-like artefact from French Polynesia, a present from Gareth, that sits on the corner of her desk.

'Is it a miniature of a ceremonial knife used for human sacrifice?' I hazard.

'No.'

'Is it the fang from an exotic animal?'

'Well, it is ivory, unfortunately. But no.'

Reveal. It's an ear-piercing device! Rest point on lobe. *Bang!*

On cue, in stomps the chancellor, slightly breathless after having flown in from Melbourne and taken breakfast with Jean-David Levitte, a former French presidential adviser and ambassador to the United Nations, and Evans' negotiating partner in the 1991 Cambodian Peace Process. He grabs my hand, apologises for taking me through the 'tradesman's entrance', and seats me at a large round table that fills half the office.

Now seventy-three, Evans was the Oxford graduate who came into the Hawke government as its thirty-nine-year-old attorney-general before quickly being demoted to Trade and Resources. Between 1988 and 1996, he was the country's celebrated foreign minister. Even in the dying days of the Hawke government in 1991, Evans kept his caucus vote behind his doomed master.

Evans is tall – 'six foot two and shrinking' – wears a tailored blue pinstriped suit, a fifties vintage gold IWC watch, and a red-and-white-striped tie from Nuremberg, where he's just returned from a human rights jury. He carries a dossier of notes on, coincidentally, Bob Hawke, for an upcoming memoir, his thirteenth book.

He slides into a chair, a vast belly threatening the tenacity of buttons four, five and six on his crisp white shirt, and asks a few questions about the motivation behind my book.

Evans then clasps his hands behind his head, and says: *'Go.'*

In 1983, was there a sense within the party, as there was in the community, that a messiah, a suntanned god made four inches taller by a beehive of meticulously whipped silver hair, had arrived?

'We felt more like that with Whitlam,' says Evans. 'Whitlam was the messiah of my generation and then Hawke was the *thank god* moment with which we put behind us the debacle of '75 and the catastrophe of all those following years. It was only eight years later and here we are back in government and ready to go and firing on all cylinders. It was exaltation, of course, *exhilaration* . . . but messiah? I don't know. The reason Hayden was knocked off in favour of Hawke was that there was just a total confidence that we would win with Hawke, whereas while we felt we should and we could win with Hayden, we were not absolutely sure, and Hawke was the icing on the cake. I remember it more as a sense of relief than anything else.'

The journalist Paul Kelly writes about women weeping in the streets in one of his first public appearances as Labor leader. Did you see similar instances? Were you yourself moved to tears?

Evans responds with a faux smile.

'Those of us who knew him better weren't quite as emotionally charged,' he says. 'I saw enough dimensions of his personality and enough of his human side to recognise that we weren't in the presence of God. We were in the presence of someone who a lot of people perceived as God, and that was very good for the party and good for the movement.'

What kind of man is Bob Hawke?

'Highly intelligent, capable, forceful, full of personality, very much the boyo, very much everybody's favourite drinking companion – although he had very short arms when it came to reaching into his own pocket. Famously so. He was engaging, opinionated, a force of nature.'

Did that impression change over the years?

'When he went off the grog, obviously, when he became prime minister. Then he quieted down a lot around the edges and was less of an over-the-top personality, which he tended to be when he was on the turps . . . When you took the grog away, he was missing a dimension or two.'

But, adds Evans, even without a crankcase topped with social lube, 'he had the same drive and energy and commitment that was there, and the same capacity to connect with anybody anywhere.'

Can you describe the dynamic between you and Hawke?

'It was a relationship of mutual support rather than any sort of intense bonding . . .'

There was no father–son thing?

'Oh no!' he says. 'With Beazley you sensed a lot more of that, the mentor relationship . . . You sensed that very, very strongly with Kim. But I was always more distant and [had a] more objective relationship rather than a subjective one.'

Was that by choice?

'No, [it was] because we didn't really have an awful lot in common. We had Oxford and we had university stuff and so on, but my instincts were more . . .' Evans pauses. 'It sounds pompous to say, but they were more cerebral, and I like reading.'

To make his point, Evans says Bob read one book a year at most, and once, when he consumed a book on the eighteenth-century British statesman Robert Walpole, 'we heard about bloody Robert Walpole about three times a week for the next two years'.

Hawke was highly intelligent, explains Evans, 'but not an intellectual in any way, shape or form, and with no particular interest in the arts. No interest at all in literature, fiction, no particular interest in history other than when suddenly the light bulb went off and something was extremely relevant . . . I had no interest whatsoever in the horses or gambling. We were basically quite different personalities but complementary personalities during a period when that mattered.'

I respond that it's interesting that a man like Hawke could be highly intelligent, a Rhodes Scholar with multiple degrees, but not be an intellectual.

'It's very common. Very common. More common than you might think, actually,' says Evans. 'Just with no basic intellectual interests. It's intriguing. That didn't stop him being quite an acute observer of international relations and he got very engaged in foreign policy issues and . . . was capable of seeing the bigger pictures and putting the story together. Highly, highly intelligent, but the nature of his interests were not really my interests. Like Beazley, he had a much greater personal enthusiasm for schmoozing, basically. Very comfortable spending long nights just schmoozing, gossiping, moving around, whereas I didn't mind doing that in particular over a meal or whatever, but I really want to get back to the grind of reading stuff and getting on top of policy issues and getting prepared for stuff. I just approach things in a different way.'

Oh, but it was such a vigorous government, I say.

Vigorous? Evans searches for a more accurate word. 'Robust,' he says. 'Though it was not one that was consistent with British traditions of decorum. But it was effective.'

Speaking of British traditions of decorum, I ask permission to read aloud a thrilling exchange between Hawke and Keating in Evans' book, *Inside the Hawke–Keating Government: A Cabinet Diary*.

Evans nods. I read:

> **Hawke snarled back: 'I was right and you were wrong and you'll always be wrong on this issue'. Keating in turn rounded back at him: 'You were fucking wrong and you'll live to regret it'. Schoolyard stuff, but they were both pale and tense and almost shaking with anger . . . it is the clearest indication I have seen for some time as to just how bad things are now, fundamentally, between them.'**

I tell Evans I'm surprised that there was such tension between Keating and Hawke so early in the famous partnership.

'Yes, but it wasn't existential,' he says. 'It was never so bad that it was dysfunctional. When you've got old bulls and young bulls in the same patch – old bull Hayden and young bull Evans, old bull Hawke and young bull Keating – that's life in politics and any institutional environment . . . I think most of us saw it as healthy rough and tumble. Scary for people who are not used to this sort of stuff but we're all pretty hardened professionals.'

On balance, who do you think has the more accurate recollection of that period? Hawke in his memoirs or Keating in his various outbursts?

'Hawke's is very self-serving and Paul's is very self-serving. The truth is always somewhere in between. Blanche's second biography of Hawke [*Hawke: The Prime Minister*] is, frankly, a disgrace. I would not take too much guidance from that. Even though she wrote the first one [*Robert J. Hawke: A Biography*] in circumstances that were fairly intimate, nonetheless it's a well-crafted serious biography; the second one that she wrote three years ago is just a work of second-rate hagiography. But, see, Hawke and Keating in retirement had reached a kind modus vivendi of mutual respect. I mean, Hawke himself had simply gotten over being rolled by Keating and Keating was not pursuing his vindication of history. They were just letting that lie and were reasonably civilised to each other when they bumped into each other on party occasions. But when Blanche published that book it really just made my hairs stand on end because it was just ridiculously *Hawke was brilliant from start to finish. Got everything right and Keating was a pain in the arse. And, you know, Keating contributed basically nothing and it was all Hawke's agenda every inch of the way.*'

When I put this to Blanche later an eyebrow arches.

'Sounds like Gareth was weaned on a pickle. *Hawke: The Prime Minister* is in no way a disgrace; it's an essay, modest in scope and design, that sets out to answer the question, 'What sort of leader was he?' It was written as an addition to the original biography, which had addressed the question everyone was asking: 'What sort of a man is he?' My publisher wanted to reissue the biography with an update about the prime ministership. I saw the opportunity to collect information for future scholars that otherwise would be irretrievable – the recollections of public servants and political staff, men (mostly) who would speak to me, but not to the media, and whose memories would be lost as they aged or died. However, when I'd finished it, there was a problem: even using the thinnest paper, it would make the biography into a brick. Louise Adler, publisher of MUP, and I talked it through and came to the conclusion that a stand-alone book was the better solution. Gareth shouldn't slam an unpretentious work intended for the use of future historians as "a disgrace". Obviously, he didn't read the preface in which I explained its purpose.'

So, who did what?

'Hawke is right that some of the early big reforms – the floating of the dollar and all that sort of stuff, which Keating has tended in retrospect to say me me me me me me – they were probably more Hawke than Keating. Hawke was a good economist and had a good sense of what needed to be done with these changes,' says Evans. 'It took Paul all of '83 to really get his head together, his act together and his full understanding of what the treasury was all about. He had a huge capacity to absorb information, argument and analysis, to cut to the quick and to communicate, and a huge capacity to work with the best and the brightest in treasury, but in that first period it was certainly more Hawke than Keating who delivered on all that really, really big stuff. As time went on, there's no question that Keating was the engine room for most of what kept on happening after that, year in and year out. Just the energy and the creativity and the advocacy brilliance that he brought to it were hugely important for the government.

'And it is true that Hawke's visible leadership on policy-type issues took a step back after that first year because he got the big ideas out there. Recovery, reconciliation, reconstruction, the summit, the social wage concept and the basic elements of that narrative were all in place in the first year and brilliantly sold. Thereafter, he got excited and obsessed with particular bits and pieces of foreign policy stuff and how he single-handedly brought an end to the apartheid regime in South Africa.'

How accurate is Hawke's claim that he played a pivotal role in the destruction of apartheid?

'Look,' says Evans, 'Bob played an important role, no doubt about it. At the heads of government meetings and on the financial sanctions issue he saw the way forward. But, you know, *"Nelson said to me, Without you, Bob . . ."* – well, that's gilding the lily a tiny bit."

At the launch of your book *Inside the Hawke–Keating Government: A Cabinet Diary*, Keating used the occasion to claim Hawke all but vanished as the country's prime minister from 1984 to 1989. How true is that?

'I don't buy into Keating's thesis that Hawke was out to lunch from 1984 onwards,' says Evans. 'But Hawke obviously was out to lunch in the '84 election.'

Which Hawke admits – finding out his daughter Rosslyn was a junkie, getting belted in the face by a cricket ball and so forth, I say.

'[The government] was on a high after having won in '83 and just thought they could coast, but I think they just lost the plot in all sorts of ways,' says Evans. 'I was shocked by the result when we didn't do as well as we thought we could and should, but he got his act together after that. Bob was never a detailed policy guy, but he did have a sense of direction, a sense of narrative about where the country should go and the story we as the Labor Party should tell, and I think that's one of his greatest contributions – that capacity to articulate a narrative . . . All great political leaders and all serious social transformers have a story which they can tell effectively to the public. It's not just ducking and weaving from one piecemeal thing to another. It's a storyline, and Hawke was very good at that.'

He persuaded the electorate that a Labor government wouldn't be shackled to the old strictures of socialism; that Labor understood the economy was as important to the country's health as any welfare program. And that it would, that it should, become the natural party of government.

'We were the ones that, before the British got anywhere near it, invented, basically, the Third Way,' says Evans. 'This combination of very dry economics, non-traditional Labor economics, combined with very warm and fuzzy social policy in the great Labor tradition, plus a very liberal internationalist foreign policy, again in the great Labor tradition.'

Evans lists the ability to convince the ACTU to restrain wages, while at the same time 'ensuring that nobody was left behind' made it a 'brilliantly conceived Labor narrative. Brilliant because it accommodated the traditional principles and values of the party to the realities of the modern techno-logical industrial age. If we just relied on the old protectionist policies and everybody in for their wage hikes, inflation-driven sort of stuff, the country was going to go out the door backwards. Bob saw this very well, whereas in Britain the Thatcherites had also seen the necessity for change and delivered it in a very thuggish and ugly way. And then Blair came along with basically the same storyline, which he picked up from Australia, which people don't fully appreciate.'

It's a matter on which Evans can speak with authority. For three days in 1990, he showed Gordon Brown and Tony Blair, both to become British Labor prime ministers, the inner work-ings of the Hawke government.

'You could see the brains going off like flashbulbs as they realised the significance of what we were doing,' says Evans. 'Forget about [British sociologist] Tony Giddens and the LSE [London School of Economics], all the other people who are supposed to be architects of the Blairite Third Way. It was really the Australian experience and what those guys learned from what Hawke and the rest of us were doing here in marrying together the dry rigorous economics with the decent social policy and decent foreign policy. The great fascination of that encounter with Blair and Brown was that everybody thought Brown was the next big thing . . .'

Oh, I can't imagine dreary Brown usurping bright-as-a-button Blair. But yes, Evans responds in splendid Latin: Brown dominated 'for ... gravitas, the pietas and the dignitas. Tony was just a little bandy skipping along in the rear. The big, bright smile and slightly goofy grin. I mean smart, but a lightweight by comparison to Gordon Brown the heavyweight.'

Combine Hawke's instinctive sense of narrative with his rock-star cabinet – 'the gold standard,' says Evans – and you have an immensely capable and effective government.

'Everything was contested, everything was contestable, and that makes for very healthy government because, provided people keep the arguments within the cabinet room ... there was a common commitment to the collective cause. If there were arguments about anything it was, "What's the best policy?" Or, "What's the best way to deliver it?" Or, "What's the best way to sell it?" There weren't arguments that were personal or ideologically driven. You didn't have that sort of jealousy-type environment, even in the later stages when the Keating–Hawke stuff got rather fraught. You always had the sense that it was the larger Labor enterprise, the larger government enterprise. Even when we finally went out of office after thirteen years, this was not a government that had fallen apart internally. It was not a government that was riven with divisions and personality squabbles or anything like that. It was a government that just got tired and people were a bit sick of us and people were ready for change.'

How do the eight years of the Hawke government compare to Howard's four-term reign – and, for that matter, the chaos of Rudd–Gillard and Abbott–Turnbull – that followed?

'It sounds ridiculous and romantic, but when you compare and contrast it, the Howard government was stable, but it was stable without any real mojo internally. They continued some of the key reforms and added to one or two of them, but there was no drive. There was no ambition. There was a much-reduced place in the world in terms of the international stuff.

'Then you get to Rudd, Gillard, Abbott, Turnbull and it's just a different universe of jealousy and personality and ideology and dysfunction and a lack of collective capacity to focus on the main game. My story about Rudd is, I think it was a tragedy that he was taken down the way he was and a tragedy that Gillard came to power that way, because it just tarnished her from the beginning.'

Evans posits that if the Rudd government (and let's remember that Rudd came into the prime minister's job with a popularity rating almost the equal of Hawke's: 74 per cent in 2008) had had a cabinet like Hawke's, the government would've soared.

'The real weakness was the inability of that collective core of other senior ministers, ten to twelve of them, to get their own act together and go to the leader and say, "Come on, buddy. Get your act together. This place is falling apart. You're running it like a bloody two-bit Napoleon,"' says Evans. 'If that message had been given with any clarity to Rudd when he first started to behave in a dysfunctional fashion and disrespectful fashion to colleagues, senior public servants, and all of the other things we know about that government, if he had got that message early on, he was smart enough to have learned that, but they were just so weak.'

In *A Cabinet Diary* you write, 'I just find Keating's conversation and company easier to take than Hawke's staccato narcissism.' What do you mean by staccato narcissism? I ask.

Well, says Evans, we must first remember that when he wrote the book he was still 'wounded' after being demoted from attorney-general to Minister for Trade and Resources.

'It was very painful and humiliating at the time, because I'd only been in the job for eighteen months and it was the job that everyone associated with me and everyone lusted for,' he says.

But caveat aside . . .

'Hawke *is* a narcissist . . . Anyone who gets to senior levels in politics, and particularly leadership levels, as I've often said, you've got to be a deeply flawed personality. You've just got

1983 WINFIELD CUP

PRIME MINISTER BOB HAWKE & PARRAMATTA CAPTAIN STEVE EDGE

To Prime Minister
Bob Hawke —
A memorable moment in History
to be shared by all.... with my very
best wishes
Gene Cernan Apollo XVII
10/18/83

The Honorable Robert Hawke
With best wishes, from your friend
Gy Bush

UNION CAMP   BARCALDINE 1891   CHAPMAN

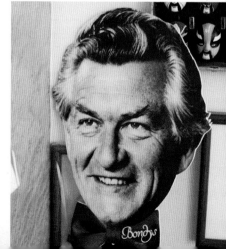

levels of insensitivity known to no ordinary mortal to survive the rigours of these sorts of jobs. You've got to be a bit psychologically different. You've got to be a bit psychologically strange to ever fight your way to the top and stay there for any period of time. Normal people don't get these jobs because normal people just get burned off along the way by the stresses and the strains and some of the indecencies of the process.'

As for Keating, Evans says he iced their friendship over a few quotes in the ABC's 2014 *Australian Story* episode on Hawke, 'Just Call Me Bob'. Evans had said, 'Bob was an absolutely brilliant prime minister and he touched every leadership base you can think of,' and, 'The notion that Bob was out of it for another four or five years after that I think is just wrong.'

Evans says now, 'That was not the narrative that Paul wants burnished into the public mind. Paul's a bit grumpy with the world because he never really found a role for himself after and still feels bitter and twisted about losing to Howard . . . He should have gone off and done something . . . If I stayed around Australia – well, you're sort of getting in the way or you're going to be miserable that you're not part of it or whatever – so I just went off overseas for a decade and ran another organisation internationally just to get out of the place. I think it would have been very sensible for Paul to do that.'

But Hawke . . .

'Nobody has a career that goes like that and then you just dribble off into the twilight of the time of your own choosing. It's a switch-back ride and the highs are fantastic and the lows are awful. The high can be fantastic again and then most people are carried out at the end of it. I don't know how many political careers end in triumph and success, with people leaving at exactly the top of their game at exactly the right time. Practically never. Most people just have to be dragged out.'

Or you die.

'Or you die,' says Evans. 'But looking back from the perspective of history, I don't think too much should be made of that, the fact that Hawke . . .' Evans reflects for a beat. 'He did go, eventually, pretty gracefully, quite frankly. Extraordinarily gracefully. But that's just the nature of the process. It's a bloody and dangerous trade.'

— CHAPTER 13 —

THE ELECTION OF DONALD TRUMP

I N NOVEMBER, THE SEVENTY-YEAR-OLD MULTIBILLIONAIRE
Donald Trump is elected as the forty-fifth president of the
United States.

A surprise?

Not to the 62 million Americans Hillary Clinton pasted as
'deplorables' and who figured a property developer with an itchy
Twitter finger and tiny little hands built for pussy-grabbing
made more sense than a former senator and Secretary of State.

It shocked the hell out of Hawke.

In our previous conversations about Trump, he'd puked
clouds of smoke from his Davidoff but told me not to fret.
'Trump's not going to become president.'

It's a far more circumspect Hawke post-election. He is five
dollars lighter after Blanche correctly called the result, which
is a thorn in his side, but the result coincides with a spike in his
health. Hawke's face is brighter, the suntan darker, his posture
upright, the eyebrows even more athletic.

It wasn't until a gossipy Sunday lunch with Blanche the week
before (*A gay prime minister? Never-revealed affairs featuring*

the most unlikely participants?) that I'd found out he'd been loaded up on the super-antibiotic Vancomicyn from September 2015 to October 2016. Doctors reserve Vancomicyn for only the most serious and life-threatening conditions – golden staph and so on. As Blanche tells it, in the middle of 2015 Hawke was lying in bed in Sydney's St Vincent Hospital, wasting away with a 'Saudi Arabian stomach bug'. A paralysed intestine. Doctors couldn't fix it. Filled him with enemas, laxatives. Didn't do a damn thing. Hawke kept losing weight. Disappearing.

'He was dying,' says Blanche. 'He had about three weeks to live. I had to let the kids know without alarming them horribly and at the same time keep it out of the media.'

Blanche described the symptoms to her own gastroentero-logist, Professor Thomas Borody, who is the founder and medical director of the Centre for Digestive Diseases in Sydney's Five Dock. (The centre describes itself as 'a unique medical institution offering novel approaches in researching, diagnosing and treating gastrointestinal (GI) conditions'.) The doc prescribed Vancomicyn; the side effects include wheezing and muscle spasms, and it costs $800 for a ten-day dose (though Borody gave Hawke the meds for free by way of a thank you for all the good he did for Australia, a gift for which the former PM is eternally grateful). The drug pulled Hawke out of his death spiral.

It's spring. Even in the late afternoon the temperature is thirty-one degrees. A thunderstorm looms out west. Hailstones. Hawke appears energised by the heat.

He rips the cigar (another Romeo y Julieta, $27) out of its plastic tube. Cuts the end. Cheeks draw. Click. Flame.

I tell him he's looking a million bucks.

'Jolly good.' Hawke grins. 'It's just the *fucking feet*. What are we on today?'

Trump.

'Let's wait a minute,' he says. 'We won a cricket match today.'

It isn't a glorious win. Australia's only victory in the three-test series against South Africa. Dead rubbers are worthless. It's an accepted fact of test cricket that the losing side picks up the final match, a crumb licked off the floor while the other side paddles your arse.

It's not exactly a golden period of Australian cricket, I say.

'It sure isn't,' says Hawke. 'You can hardly get interested in it these days.'

Hawke switches to the right-wing machinations within the Liberal party aimed at destabilising the prime minister, Malcolm Turnbull. Each day brings a new swing from Tony Abbott, the sitting prime minister he sank. It has echoes of Keating in 1991; of Rudd in 2012.

'Malcolm's got a problem – a real problem,' says Hawke. 'He was thinking about joining the Labor Party when they lost the referendum on the republic . . . He's not by conviction a Liberal. To get the leadership he had to give up some positions he really believed in. I'm not trying to denigrate him. My view of Malcolm is he's ashamed of himself for what he's done in terms of compromising his beliefs to get the numbers against Abbott. And if you're ashamed of yourself that's not a very good basis for leadership. It's a very difficult position to find yourself in.'

Hawke smacks a cloud. Leans back.

'So many people in the Liberal Party, both in the parliament and outside, just don't regard him as a Liberal. I don't say this with any pleasure or animosity at all. Just an objective statement. If there was someone standing there I think they'd knock him off. But they just don't have the depth of talent.'

Julie Bishop?

A possibility, but 'her weakness is economics and that's disastrous in a prime minister'.

Like Gough?

'The one great flaw with Gough was his lack of interest in economics,' Hawke agrees. 'He almost had sort of fear of it.'

Just before the 1972 election that ended twenty-three years of conservative rule, Hawke pulled Gough aside and said, 'Mate, you're going to win and you're going to do some great things socially and internationally.' *But.* 'Your government will live or die on how you handle the economy.'

Hawke offered to arrange for Australia's best economists from the ANU to give the new prime minister a crash-course in economics over a few weeks. Hawke knew a man of Gough's intellectual heft could easily absorb complicated theories. And as he told Gough, 'The basics are not terribly difficult.'

So what happened?

'Once he got in, I couldn't get him,' says Hawke. 'He just wouldn't do it. And so you had the fiasco of the loans affair and all that nonsense. That was a great tragedy because he was a great, great leader in so many ways, did so many great things, but my prognosis was absolutely right. His absence of interest in economics was, in the end, what brought the government down.'

As a man who loves Australia, do you believe we are being competently led?

'No . . . Education is fundamentally important. The Liberals are not sufficiently committed to the necessary levels of expenditure and prioritising. This is fundamental in determining the future quality of the country.

'If you go back just a few years, I've mentioned Iraq. This was a terrible decision. All the United States intelligence agencies said that it was one of the worst decisions that had ever been made by an American president. We just went along with it automatically as we had with Vietnam, which made such a joke of the myth which they seek to perpetrate. [The Liberals] are the ones that you can trust for looking after the security of the country? They got thrown out at the beginning of the Second World War because they couldn't handle the defence of the country. They did Vietnam, didn't learn from that, and then they did Iraq. The world is still paying an enormous price for that ghastly mistake. I don't want to be a knocker. Again, that's not basically my nature. I try to be objective about these things. I think when you look at education and social welfare, equality of opportunity, I think these things are not as strong in our national structure now as they have been and should be.'

If Beazley had won in 2001, would Australia have gone to Iraq?

'No!' snaps Hawke.

(Beazley is more pragmatic. 'The question would have arisen, what do you do? The decision's been taken, you've opposed it, but the Americans are going to go anyway. What do you do?' he asks rhetorically. 'You stand down? I probably would have just said, "We've got a couple of ships in the Persian Gulf, they're now rebadged. They are escorts for whatever American carrier battle group is there and that's it." I don't think I would have left the Americans with absolutely nothing and just hanging out to dry.')

Back to Hawke. How would Australia be different if we hadn't gone to Iraq?

'It's not just Australia, it's the world. We lost lives. Any life lost on a bad political decision is disastrous,' he says. 'An enormous amount of money was spent, which could have been otherwise spent on education, for instance. The world would be a more secure place if we hadn't gone into Iraq. They strengthened the hand of the terrorists beyond measure.'

Hawke bends the conversation back to the Liberal leadership. Is there a possibility that Abbott might return? I ask.

'They won't go back to Tony. He'd like to. I like Tony personally, but he was somewhat bizarre as prime minister. That problem with Prince Philip [when Abbott granted the Queen's husband a knighthood]. Just unbelievable. Where did that come from?'

He is trying hard, though, Mr Hawke.

'Yeah, he's fucking around behind the scenes.'

Hawke grabs his large cappuccino, foam generously decorated with three hits of powdered chocolate and some crushed Flake, and takes a swig. The plastic lid isn't fixed properly and he winds up with drops of coffee on his pale blue button-up. For a moment, he has the sartorial flair of his former defence minister Kim Beazley.

'I made a nice mess of my shirt,' says Hawke.

He tips the rest of the coffee over the edge of the balcony. 'Handy bin this.'

'Now,' he says. 'Let's get started.'

Trump, I say. Is it an American tragedy?

'I do cryptic crosswords and I said, it's the beginning of the end, the end is rump. *Trump.* Look, if he were to govern according to his campaign performance it would be an unmitigated disaster, but he won't. There's an enormous obligation upon leaders in the rest of the world to hold their hand out and try to cooperate with him.'

What relationships are most important to the United States?

'The most important relationship in the world is between China and the United States. I've spent a lot of time with the Chinese, you know that. I've told you about the China Institute for International Strategic Studies, which is under the auspices of China's PLA [People's Liberation Army]. I speak with them a lot, lecture to them. I told them in discussions that Hillary would win and that I'd written to Hillary wishing her luck and told her about China. I told her I hoped to speak to her about it. She indicated she would like to. I obviously can't do that now, but I'll see if I can organise a meeting with Trump. Greg [Norman, the golfer who organised a call between Turnbull and Trump immediately post-election] is a friend of mine.'

You and the Shark swing clubs together?

'Oh yes, I've played golf with Greg.'

(An aside: Hawke tells me he has nailed three holes-in-one in thirty years of strolling the greens. Two at Bonnie Doon, one in Canberra.

Any witnesses?

'*Plenty* of witnesses,' says Hawke.)

Back to the new president.

'I'm going to try to talk to Trump and reassure him about the Chinese. The Chinese are not a hegemonic power. They have not been historically and they're not now. They don't make any claims to the South China Sea. What I've suggested to them is that they should convene a meeting, which they would chair, of the interested parties in the South China Sea and try to establish a regime for joint development.'

How do the Chinese feel about it?

'They're responsive to the idea.'

The Chinese, I believe, value predictability. Do you think the capricious nature of Donald Trump will pose a problem?

'Of course it does,' says Hawke. 'It depends upon his intention. If I can persuade him that it's in his interest and America's interest, and that he could achieve something that's never been done before, well, this could be attractive to him.'

Do you think it's the end of the United States' role as the world's super cop? Trump's been isolationist in his policies, on the stump at least. Is it the end of Pax Americana?

'Pax Americana has been a bit of a myth for a while now,' says Hawke.

Still, Bush had his dream of spreading the glories of democracy to the Middle East and Obama kept at least one hand on his pistol: drones over Yemen, Somalia and Pakistan; a presence in Afghanistan. What would be the repercussions if America pulled back from NATO, from Japan, from South Korea?

'I hope he doesn't push ahead with the concept of Japan and South Korea getting nuclear arms. We don't want to see the spread of nuclear weapons. Another thing I would like to tell Trump is that the critical factor in containing North Korea is China. It's a matter I think it would be worth him talking with the Chinese about.'

If you were the prime minister, would you have immediately engaged like Turnbull?

'Yeah, immediately. Every world leader should say, "We didn't support your campaign, but you are the democratically elected leader of the second-biggest nation in the world, the second-biggest economy now. What you do and how you behave is important for everyone and we want to help you." That's what the approach ought to be. That's certainly what I would do.'

What's your opinion of Hillary's campaign?

'Trump tapped into a mood. She didn't really tap into anything. The thing that surprised me is that so many American women could have voted for Trump after the things he said about women.'

It's interesting, I note, that Trump's campaign was regarded as divisive and yet Hillary threw down the identity politics card which, by its nature, is archly divisive.

'She didn't distinguish herself,' says Hawke.

How would you have campaigned?

'I certainly would have gone to more states and I would have acknowledged the fact that America has become a very unequal society and I'd promise to do something about that.'

Do you believe Hillary lacked the ability to create a narrative Americans could relate to?

'Yeah, I do. She didn't have the narrative that great leaders have. Trump's narrative was Make America Great Again. And he repeated it over and over again.'

How did you feel, watching the election on television and seeing the needle swing towards Trump?

Hawke sighs. He puts down his cigar. The wise grandfather explaining to the naive boy one of life's truths.

'The thing is,' says Hawke, 'there's no point in getting upset and –' he waves his arms theatrically – '*oh shit* . . . It's a fact of life and you've got to deal with it. It's very simple. You've got to be pragmatic.'

How would you compare the election of Ronald Reagan, who was also ridiculed for being a right-wing simpleton, to Trump?

'Reagan was a very considerable man,' says Hawke. 'I told you the story of our first meeting with the cards?'

He had. But it's a doozy. Tell me again.

'It's worth telling.' He laughs. 'The first congratulatory message I got from any international leader when I won was from Reagan. And that was because George Shultz, who was his Secretary of State, was a very close friend of mine. George told Reagan that I was a great guy. And so Reagan said he wanted me to come over as soon as I could.'

This was June 1983. Reagan and Hawke met in the White House. They sat opposite each other, Hawke with his people on one side, Reagan with Shultz and the rest on the other.

Reagan welcomed Hawke, told everyone he was a hell of a man, then said, 'Well, Bob, perhaps you'd like to start off the discussion.'

America was just coming out of a mild recession so Hawke asked what the likely rate of economic growth was over the course of the next couple of years.

Reagan had a stack of cards in his hands. He flicked through until he reached one that said ECONOMY. He turned to his Secretary of the Treasury, Don Regan, and said, 'Perhaps you'd like to take this up with Bob.'

The president said nothing while Hawke and Regan engaged. When the conversation wrapped up, Reagan said, 'That was mighty interesting, Bob. What would you like to ask next?'

Hawke told him he wanted to discuss international affairs.

Reagan riffled through the stack for the card that read INTERNATIONAL AFFAIRS, turned to George Shultz and said, 'Perhaps you'd like to take this up with Bob.'

'And so the whole thing went on,' says Hawke. 'The most powerful man in the world sits there and says nothing. But what would you rather have? A bloke who doesn't really know anything about the subject rabbiting on or a serious discussion? He must always be remembered as a very considerable president because he didn't pretend to be well-read and well-versed in all the things he had to deal with, but he picked good people and he relied on them. In all my visits – I made about five visits – not once did I meet anyone on either side of politics who didn't like him personally. I was meeting with the speaker of the house. He said, "I see you've been down to the White House already." I said yes, I had a meeting with Ron. He said, "He's the most conservative bastard that's ever been in the White House but you can't help liking the guy." Which was indicative. Within his intellectual limitations he was a considerable leader.'

Hawke says Ronald Reagan was so fond of him he asked him to regale the official dinner with his wit. Hawke told a ribald gag about an archbishop catching his thumb on a rose's thorn. The punchline – 'And then Alice leaned across and said to His Grace, *Is your prick still throbbing?*' – was a great hit.

'It was summer and the waiters were marines dressed in

their beautiful white uniforms,' Hawke recalls. 'We each had a marine serving us. The one that was serving Reagan was one of the most handsome men I've ever seen. He was black, beautifully built, about six foot one or two. All of a sudden he couldn't control himself and he burst out laughing. And Ronald turns around and says, "It was a good one wasn't it?"'

I ask Hawke if he's heard of the conservative political commentator Glenn Beck (he hasn't). I read aloud Beck's remarks to *The New Yorker*, describing Trump as 'dangerously unhinged' and criticising American culture for embracing the baddies. He lampoons the problem with a reference to the cult TV show, *The Sopranos*: 'I love Tony Soprano. But when a Tony Soprano shows up in your life, you don't love him so much.'

How do you respond? I ask.

'America is in bad shape, there's no doubt about that. The inequality that's developed is destabilising. You can understand why people responded to a man who was saying "I'm going to make America great again", because they don't feel great.'

Do you think it's a reflection of modern celebrity culture?

'Yeah, that's part of it,' says Hawke.

What is your opinion of the current state of western culture? Is it on a high or are we part of a long, slow car crash?

'You've got to read everything in the light of this enormous threat of ISIS terrorism. The world is frightened and their entitled to be frightened. The real concern I have is that they get their hands on a nuclear device. If they do, who knows what could happen? I don't think you can say that the state of society, culture, means we're as well-equipped as we would like to be to deal with this threat.'

You're fond of saying, 'change the government and you change the country.' How do you see America changing?

'Some of the early signs are promising in that he does seem to be prepared to listen to people who are prepared to talk to him in a constructive manner,' says Hawke. 'I'm not as pessimistic as one felt and thought when he got there. I think he will be a much better president than he was a candidate.'

Is it conceivable that Trump may be a more effective president than Obama? The Republicans have the majority of state governorships and they control Congress, so they won't be as choked as the Democrats. Is it possible, despite your misgivings and the fears of millions of others, that *good* things could happen?

'One of the things that won't be good is these appointments of justices to the Supreme Court and the possibility that you'll get a reversion of decisions like Roe v. Wade,' says Hawke. 'That's bit of a concern.'

Keating talked about leaders needing a crazy gene to make a difference. Do you agree?

'Just a minute . . . *fuck*.' (Cigar ash drops into his lap.) 'No, I don't think so.'

How do you feel about the worldwide swing to the right? Marine Le Pen in France, Geert Wilders in the Netherlands, Trump in the US. Does it feel a little like the 1930s all over again, the rise of a new form of fascism?

'I don't think it's as bad as that. I mean, you haven't got a Hitler. Of course, the worrying person is Putin.'

Why does Putin worry you?

'Because he wants to recreate the Soviet Union . . . which is not a good thing.'

Is there some justification for Russia's fears given that NATO has pushed so far against its borders?

'NATO was the worst thing in that respect,' says Hawke. 'It gave him some ground to say, well, look, you're crowding me and I'm going to react.'

It's been reported that Xi Jinping was relieved that Hillary was defeated. Is there a possibility that Trump could actually drive a wedge between China and Russia, given Trump's supposed friendship with Putin?

'You've got to remember that China regarded Russia, justifiably, as a hell of a threat in the Soviet period,' says Hawke. 'They don't love Russia.'

What dangers do you believe Australia faces in the coming years, socially, economically, globally?

'I think it's almost inevitable that we're going to suffer a terrorist attack here in Australia,' says Hawke. 'It's almost beyond belief that we won't because we are very active in the fight against ISIS. Of course, I hope that I'm wrong, but I doubt that I am. We need to be very, very strong in our security arrangements. The real danger in the world, however, is that these terrorist groups get their hands on a nuclear device. And we've got to be realistic: it's a possibility. You know the American political thriller writer Richard North Patterson?'

The stud who wrote *Balance of Power*? Who makes you feel as if the world is going to go up in flames at any second?

'Yeah, did you read *The Devil's Light*? It's about terrorists.'

Getting nukes?

'Yep, getting nukes. It's worth a read. This goes back to things we've talked about before. We just need world leaders who are going to face up to all these harsh realities. Economically, there's absolutely no doubt the one thing we've got to do is take the world's nuclear waste. It is just a no-brainer. Every scientist, and any political scientist who knows anything about it, accepts and understands that nuclear-generated power is an essential part of dealing with the threats of global warming. The only difficulty, or major problem about this, is the disposal of nuclear waste.'

Hawke's big on Australia becoming a storage facility for the world's nuclear waste. In 2016, South Australia's Nuclear Fuel Cycle Royal Commission agreed, finding that the risks were manageable and that Australia had an ethical responsibility to other countries to take their radioactive waste.

It's not a new idea for Hawke. He's been pushing it for nearly thirty years.

'When I was prime minister, just towards the very end, I got my chief scientist, Professor Ralph Slatyer, to establish a committee of world experts in mining and geology to look at where were the safest sites in the world. Without any doubt, the safest sites were in Australia. And they identified Western Australia, the Northern Territory and South Australia.'

Hawke's so passionate about getting the world's nukes in the Australian dirt he's even willing to throw the idea at those least likely to embrace it. At the Woodford Folk Festival in 2016, he told his audience, 'The time has come when we've got to think big if we're going to face the big issues of our time. We're going to have to be prepared to think about changes that are quite radical.'

The crowd of wannabe radicals applauded like hell. *Radical!* They liked where Hawke was going. Then he hit them with the hammer. *Nuclear power* was the future. And Australia, as a good global citizen and net exporter of energy, should take the world's spent nuclear fuels.

'Nuclear power would be a win for the environment and an essential part of the attack that must be made on this grievous and dangerous global warming. It would be a win for the global environment and a win for Australia . . . What is worse for our kids and their kids? Some nuclear accidents in their time or the destruction of the planet [via climate change]?'

The poor partygoers in their fairy dresses and balloon pants and rainbow top hats didn't know what to think. Nukes: bad. Fixing global warming: good. Hawke had them in a spin.

Some applauded. Some yelled, 'No thanks!'

But as the *New York Times* reports in March 2017 under the headline STRUGGLING WITH JAPAN'S NUCLEAR WASTE SIX

YEARS AFTER DISASTER, the permanent removal of radioactive waste is a worldwide problem.

It's been six years since three reactors melted down at the Fukushima Daiichi Nuclear Power Station, following the devastating earthquake and tsunami of 2011. Yet, as the report explains, Japanese officials are still debating how to deal with an 'ever-growing pile of radioactive waste'. Some authorities propose diluting contaminated water and dumping it into the ocean, but face vehement opposition from local fishermen. And while 3.5 billion gallons of radioactive soil has been collected for incineration (so far), this will only serve to reduce the harmful waste rather than eradicate it.

If the Japanese do dump the tainted water into the ocean, where does that leave the world's fisheries? How does it affect the Pacific?

Hawke is adamant that the solution lies with Australia.

'We've got the world's safest sites. We've got an obligation to make those available,' he says. 'And, of course, it transforms our revenue situation because the world will be willing to pay large amounts. On one of my recent visits in China, I met the previous Japanese prime minister, [Yasuo] Fukuda, and I told him about it, and he nearly had an orgasm about the thought of being able to clear their waste. I think both parties realise that now, and I think Turnbull is starting to move towards it. I've spoken to him before about how I thought it was fundamental. He didn't disagree. The Labor Party will have to support it.'

How do you sell that to the electorate? The thought of Australia becoming a garbage bin for radioactive waste gives me the shivers.

'If we have the safest sites in the world, and it could be done without any threat of danger to Australia ... "Not in my backyard" – well, the point is we've got the world's biggest bloody backyard. And the safest.'

A viability analysis by the Royal Commission found that a 'waste disposal facility could generate more than $100 billion income in excess of expenditure' over the course of 120 years. Would it be that transformative for the economy?

'It totally changes the revenue that we have,' says Hawke. 'The whole debate has been sort of two-legged instead of three-legged. You have cuts in expenditure, you increase taxes, or you get a new source of revenue.'

Of course, none of it – global warming, the use of nuclear power, Australia's deserts being underground repositories of phenomenally toxic waste – means a damn thing if Trump, in a fit of pique at China or Iran or North Korea, pushes the button and wipes us all out.

We spoke earlier about countries being at certain points economically and culturally as seasons. Do you think America, with Trump as leader, is in its winter?

'Now,' says Hawke, 'I don't think that's a useful sort of analogy. It's in a Trump season at the moment and we have yet to see how that works out.'

Hawke stubs his cigar out. Blows a final plume of smoke. Interview over.

— CHAPTER 14 —

JOHN HOWARD

AUSTRALIA'S SECOND-LONGEST-SERVING PRIME MINISTER, three years longer at the wheel than Hawke, pulls up a chair in front of me, spreads his legs and plants his hands on his thighs.

The Honourable John Howard, OM, AC (who isn't particularly short, if you were wondering, despite wearing the pejorative Little Johnny tag through every election cycle since 1987), is immaculately dressed in a navy pinstriped suit with a white shirt and dazzling gold cufflinks, a red tie and high-sheen black shoes.

It's been a circuitous route to get to his office. Two days earlier, my telephone rang while I was driving. I glanced at the screen. Private number. Who picks up a private call? It's either a telemarketer or some kind of overseas scam.

Hello, my friend! Can I first get your bank account number and date of birth?

I'd thrown the phone back on the passenger seat.

A few minutes later it hit again.

The caller was clearly determined. My curiosity was piqued, so I picked up.

I missed the caller's name. Something about an appointment on Thursday. Would I mind *terribly*, uh, would it be *too much of an inconvenience,* if the interview was changed to the following day? Same time, of course. The caller was disarmingly polite, the voice a little older than that of my usual pals.

An appointment on Thursday morning. Older, well-spoken male.

The penny dropped with a clang.

The voice was suddenly, overwhelmingly, familiar.

John Howard.

The PM who took the guns off the streets and boldly loosed East Timor from the yoke of Indonesia ('A terrible international humiliation for Indonesia,' says Howard) and who responded to the Bali bombings with the statesmanlike call to 'wrap our arms not only around our fellow Australians but our arms around the people of Indonesia, of Bali'.

This was also the man who warned Australia about Asian immigration and plied the narrative that a boatful of Iraqis had tossed their kids into the ocean to provoke a rescue, and asylum, who recoils at the idea of homosexuals sashaying down the aisle, who took us into Iraq on the lap of baby Bush and who was the first PM to be turfed out of office and, simultaneously, his own seat since Stanley Baldwin in 1929.

A rock star to the Libs; the devil, if you're on the left.

I'd fawned, naturally.

Around the dinner table we might talk tough. We hurl invective at the television, mutter at the newspaper, complain darkly about the stupidity and the greed of politicians. But when you have John Howard calling you on your own phone, it's not as if you're going to be rude. It speaks volumes about Howard's character that he isn't too self-important to jump on the phone and change an appointment.

'Mr Howard? Is that you? Yes, yes, you tell me what time.'

As for the relationship between Hawke, the elder by ten-and-a-half years, and Howard, it had always hovered between a begrudging respect and the political need to nail the other against a wall.

When the pair met at the National Press Club in 2012 for an interview with Ray Martin, it was as if Martin and Dean had reunited. Political vaudeville ensued.

Hawke prefixes a question with, 'I don't know if John will agree with me . . .'

'Just try me!' interrupts Howard.

Hawke retorts: 'I've been trying you for a *long* time . . .'

Later . . .

Howard: 'Undeniably, Menzies was the greatest prime minister. *Undeniably.*'

Hawke interjects: 'I deny it.'

The crowd whoops.

Hawke: 'Why did they throw him out?'

Howard: 'Why did they throw him out? Well, *your mob threw you out!*'

Hawke throws his hands up in mock defeat. 'I know! I know!'

Good friends, says Hawke. But there are caveats. Lines like 'I *essentially* agree with Bob' and 'John is *basically* honest' get thrown around a lot.

When I'd told Hawke I'd be swinging by Howard, he said, 'John will be interesting. He's always been very generous. I can't be quite as generous in return [though] I speak well of him. He was an absolutely dedicated Tory and probably the most resilient politician we've ever had. He's a considerable figure. He was a very good prime minister in many ways. The three things that I can never forgive him for were the Asian thing, Kids Overboard and his unqualified support for the invasion of Iraq.'

Two days after Howard's call, I'm about to ascend to the fifty-third floor of a Sydney skyscraper for our 11.30 interview when the phone rings. Private. I know to pick up. It's Howard's secretary.

'Oh, Mr Rielly, I'm so sorry but something very important has come up. Would you mind . . .'

My heart sinks.

'. . . changing the appointment to 11.45? Mr Howard is so sorry, but he has to take this call.' A torrent of apologies – if it's too difficult, he can change it; he's terribly sorry etc.

Just as I settle back into the leather cushions of the building's lobby, peeling open my phone to re-watch the Howard–Hawke interview on Menzies, a call comes through.

'Actually, he just finished. Is it okay if you come now?'

A wooden doorframe with frosted glass. A small button. Immediately, the door swings open and I'm greeted by a well-pressed man in his fifties who introduces himself as Stuart.

'I'm Mr Howard's driver,' he says. Do I want water? Tea?

The secretary ducks her head in to ask if I'm okay, also offers tea, apologises again – Mr Howard has another call and he'll be five or so minutes.

I wander through the office and check out the sporting memorabilia room. Howard's driver plays tour guides. We chit-chat a little.

I say that he must have been front row to more than a few significant individuals in his decade driving Howard around. Photos of Howard with world leaders are displayed on bookshelves that flank the two chairs in the waiting room. There's Howard with Margaret Thatcher, with George W. Bush (not on lap), with Pakistani military president Pervez Musharraf, with Israel's Ehud Barak, meeting Pope Benedict XVI, the Queen, Tony Blair, Bill Clinton. And so on.

The driver laughs. 'Not really. I see a lot of underground carparks.'

What kind of car does a man of Howard's stature and career warrant?

For the past ten years it's been a Holden Calais, I'm told, but since the old lion is winding down its production in Australia there've been a few good deals happening, and Howard's been upgraded to the slightly bigger Caprice.

'Janette likes the extra leg room,' he says.

Now, if you were to imagine John Howard's post-prime ministerial office, you'd include a room for cricket memorabilia, accents of dark wood, views of Sydney Harbour and maybe a couple of framed newspaper front pages celebrating Howard's five election victories (HOWARD TRIUMPHANT, LANDSLIDE CRUSHES ALP). Prints of the doomed World War II vessel HMAS *Sydney* (II) (sunk in 1941, 645 sailors killed) and Cook's HM *Bark Endeavour*, painted by the ninety-three-year-old Australian naval artist Oswald Brett, hang on facing walls.

Of greater patriotic interest is the cricket room, with its bin full of Prime Minister XI bats, a line-up of various other souvenir bats leaning against a wall, including a 1948 Don Bradman Invincibles bat and a bat decorated with an Aboriginal dot painting. A framed photo of Sir Robert Menzies in 1951 with the West Indian cricket team is, says Howard's driver, the photo most examined by visitors.

Arranged on the other walls and in a display cabinet are the famous photo of Steve Waugh, arms outstretched after his last-ball century against England at the SCG in 2003, Howard with Mark Taylor, with Ian Thorpe, with John Bertrand, Dawn Fraser and – ah, yes – his old adversary Bob Hawke.

As if on cue, I see Howard enter the waiting room, his secretary hurrying behind him.

'Where's Mr Rielly?' he booms.

I move out of his blind spot. We shake – such a *vital* grip – and Howard, who is seventy-seven years old but bounces with the vigour of someone who animates his body regularly, leads me the few metres into his apartment-sized office. Fifty-three floors above Sydney Harbour, the visitor and his master are bathed in the light from a floor-to-ceiling window that stretches the twenty-metre length of the office.

The eastern and western walls feature floor-to-ceiling book-cases. A large dark wood desk occupies the western quarter, a small lounge and a chair are on the opposite side, and there is a lectern in the middle with the day's newspapers neatly arranged. It so happens that Mike Baird has just resigned as NSW premier.

The headlines read:

BREAKING BAIRD

BAIRD BOWS OUT

BRUISED BAIRD BAILS.

'Seven premiers in ten years,' I say.

'And this was a good one,' muses Howard.

Howard takes up the lounge chair. I'm on the leather couch, which is slightly lower, thereby allowing the former PM a superior position.

I ask Howard to describe his current relationship with Hawke. Well, he says, they don't exactly seek each other out. But they have appeared together at various public events sixty-ish times.

'There's no point in maintaining any sort of personal antagonism,' says Howard.

What are your early memories of Hawke?

'He was very much the outspoken, sometimes belligerent trade union leader,' says Howard. 'I remember the very first time I had to deal with him one-on-one...'

A landline rings.

'Excuse me for a moment. *Tony... Could I call you back? I'm just doing an interview... No, no, no, I'll ring you back, okay? Thank you.*'

Did my interview just triumph over a phone call from Tony Abbott? Howard's courtesy knows no bounds!

He continues: 'I was a very junior minister in the Fraser government and we were introducing some legislation, which I thought was long overdue, to expose trade unions to penalties if they engaged in secondary boycotts of companies. Because under the then law, if a company engaged in a secondary boycott against another company it would be penalised, and I couldn't see why a union should be any different. And what was happening was . . . say a union was having an argument with a company, they would, in order to further their argument, impose a boycott on a third company that was doing business with the company that they had the argument with.'

The turbulent seventies!

'Yeah, and we thought that was unreasonable. Bob said it was outrageous and I didn't understand industrial reality and said there'd be blood on the streets if I went ahead with it. We went ahead with it and it was legislated.'

Did Pitt Street run red with the blood of the worker?

'There wasn't any blood on the streets,' Howard says with a laugh. 'But he played his part. You could tell that he was performing on a larger stage and he did establish an identity. Whatever people's politics might have been at the time, whether they were Labor or Coalition, he did establish an identity as a major public figure long before he entered parliament.'

I say that I've read conflicting accounts of the Coalition's response to the ALP's switch to Hawke in 1983. In some accounts, Fraser said that he wasn't particularly bothered about facing Hawke in an election. In other versions, the prevailing reason for wanting that early election in '82 was so that he didn't have to face Hawke. And that after Hayden saw off Hawke's July '82 challenge the cabinet broke into spontaneous applause. What's your memory of the event?

'When Hawke became leader of the Labor Party that made our task that much harder. I'm not saying that it was impossible for Hayden to have beaten Fraser – he might've – but I thought the elevation of Hawke probably put it beyond doubt.'

Does he remember the mood surrounding Hawke's elevation to the leadership in 1983? I mention Paul Kelly's description of women weeping in the street during Hawke's first walk-through in Brisbane, adding Gareth Evans' remark, 'We were in the presence of someone who a lot of people perceived as God.'

A tight grin. 'Yeah, well,' says Howard. 'I didn't share those views.'

There was a newspaper headline in 1983 that read 'Hawke. Sexy. Tamie'. Do you remember that?

'I do,' says Howard.

Do you remember Mr Fraser or the party's reaction to it?

Curtly: 'No.'

But you could see the public adored him.

Howard nods, concedes the point. 'I didn't buy into it, but I understood it. He's an intelligent man with the common touch. He did it well, but I don't know that I was overwhelmed by it. I respected the political reality of it.'

Still, says Howard, it doesn't matter who you are. 'In the end, nobody has popularity that lasts forever. It's one of the great ironies of politics.'

I issue a language warning. Before the interview, I'd pondered the repercussions if I were to say *cunt* in the course of reciting a John Singleton quote relevant to the manner in which Howard left office. Would the great conservative leader, who values politeness above all, have me removed?

I roll my eyes to indicate I don't really want to dirty our atmospherics with gutter language but, you know how it is ... *Singo*.

Howard shrugs back to indicate we'll probably both survive the onslaught of filth.

I read aloud: *'No quivering of the bottom lip like that wuss Fraser. No self-important speeches like with Gough and these other cunts. Fucking cop it on the chin and move on.'*

Do you believe Hawke exited with similar dignity?

'He was, of course, removed by his party. I was removed by my ultimate masters, the people. I thought Hawke, when he lost the second challenge to Keating, behaved quite well.'

Howard says the first and only time he entered the prime minister's office in the new Parliament House, until he was elected himself in 1996, was shortly after Keating's coup.

'[Hawke] was there, nobody else – I think there was just one of his aides there – and he had one bit of paper on his desk.'

What was on this mysterious sheet of paper?

Howard said he couldn't see it.

(The following day, I'll have a brief email exchange with Blanche.

Me: *Would it be too much to ask your gorgeous husband if he recalls this single sheet of paper and what it was?*

B: *I'll ask him when he returns to the house this afternoon. Wonderfully mysterious.*

Later:

B: *I've just asked himself. He said, 'I've no fucking idea.' You could perhaps put that more elegantly.*

Howard, more than anyone, could relate to Hawke's pain. He was offed by Peacock after losing the '87 election to Hawke.

'I had no argument with him, and when you're removed like that . . .' Howard pauses. 'Party room removals can be very tough because there's an element of . . .'

Treachery?

Worse, says Howard. 'There's an element of regicide in it.'

From the perspective of opposition, how did you see the Keating challenges and Keating's destabilisation of the government?

'He was obviously intent on pulling it all down. I wondered about the wisdom of the Labor Party getting rid of Hawke in favour of Keating because, relatively speaking, Hawke was so very popular. But Keating won the 1993 election, and could Hawke have won it? We'll never know.'

Was it interesting to study and watch unfold?

'Oh, it was very interesting. It was taking place in a time when John Hewson was leader of the Coalition and we were doing very well in the polls and so forth. Very interesting to watch.'

With each twist of the knife, each wound opened, were there smiles in the shadow cabinet?

'No. Enough of us had been around long enough to know that these things could change very rapidly.'

Whose version of history is closer to the truth regarding the Hawke government's economic reforms, Keating's or Hawke's?

'They wouldn't ever have carried the changes with the public without Hawke,' says Howard. 'They both believed in the change. Hawke's popularity and political skills were necessary. But that is not to denigrate Keating's contribution as treasurer. People should not accept that Hawke did not have a well-developed understanding of economics. He was very good.'

As treasurer in the Fraser government, Howard had championed a dollar loosed onto the international markets, deregulating the financial system, tariff reform and running surplus budgets by hacking into welfare spending. Did he ever feel as if the Hawke government was stealing from his economic playbook?

'I think it was a deliberate policy on the part of Bob Hawke to embrace certain policies that he not only thought were good but that he also knew would be very hard for us to oppose because they were policies I, in particular, had advocated.'

Did you feel vindicated when the Hawke government floated the dollar?

'I don't know whether I felt vindicated or not. I remember supporting it. That was probably the biggest decision that that government took on the economy and I said it was correct. Correct and courageous ... There were many people on my side of politics at the time that were opposed to a float and their argument was that the Australian economy was too small and would be buffeted if we had a floating exchange rate. I didn't think that. Hawke was probably more influential in bringing about the float than Keating. Although Keating now argues that he was in favour of it ... My sense is that the then governor of the Reserve Bank, Bob Johnston, and Bob Hawke were the two people who played a dominant role in the decision to float.'

The gradual privatisation of the Commonwealth Bank by the ALP must've stuck in your craw, I suggest to Howard. Hawke called your plan to sell it off as 'economic vandalism'.

'He said it was vandalism and a Thatcherite obscenity. Oh, yes, he did all of that. He was *shameless*! He made speeches to the Labor Party faithful saying he'd never flog off the family's silver like that dreadful fellow Howard.'

In your book *The Menzies Era*, you call it a 'masterclass in political hypocrisy'.

'Yeah, of course it was.'

It's a great line.

'It's absolutely a masterclass of political hypocrisy.'

Do you believe Hawke gradually came around to the idea of privatisation of public assets or do you believe he was an opportunist?

'Both Hawke and Keating, particularly, believed they'd struck gold because I attacked them from the right, and not from the left. So they could always say, "Well, they're more extreme than we are and therefore we're the safe option."'

A smart play, says Howard. 'If they felt they had to adjust policy, they knew that given the position I had taken, I couldn't oppose them doing it.'

Tell me about the afternoon when Kim Beazley came to see you to sew up your support for the final sale of the Commonwealth Bank . . .

'Ah, Beazley, yeah. On the eve of the very last budget of the Labor government in 1995, Beazley rang me. I have always enjoyed, and continue to enjoy, a very friendly relationship with Beazley. He is a very able man. And likeable. He rang me and said, "John, is it still your policy to privatise the Commonwealth Bank?" I said, "Yeah, it's been our policy for years, for a decade." Well, he said, "We've included the privatisation of the part of the Commonwealth Bank that we still own in the budget tonight and we're counting the proceeds and it's a big part of the budget. We will need your help to get it through the Senate. Because the Democrats are opposed to it, and they hold the balance of power, and if you oppose it, we'll not get it through."

'And I said, "Well, it's our policy, we're not going to oppose it." I said, "We might highlight your bleeding hypocrisy and the fact that your treasurer promised the finance sector unions that you wouldn't do it. But we're not going to vote against something that's been our policy for ten years."'

Howard leans forward. Hands grip the thighs tight. He looks at me. It would be intimidating if I wasn't enjoying his candour so much.

'Now that was a classic example of how they needed us. And the fact that we had adopted positions, you might say to the right of where they were, made life easy for them . . . It would've been ridiculous to have opposed something just for the sake of embarrassing them. Years ago there was a case in New South Wales where the Liberal Party in opposition opposed the privatisation of some electricity assets. That was a mistake, because if you believe in something, even though the other side proposes it, you really have to accept it.'

The golden days of bipartisanship – although Keating's recollection is slightly different. In an article for *The Australian* in 2007, Keating lambasted John Howard for continuing to perpetuate 'the lie' that the Hawke and Keating governments had benefitted from opposition support for the reform agenda. 'Bob Hawke and I needed John Howard's endorsements for our policy changes in 1983 like we needed a dose of rabies.'

Speaking of Keating, the treasurer fought hard for a 12.5 per cent consumption tax in 1985. Hawke opposed it. It was the first crack in the famous relationship. Eight years later, Keating leveraged public fear of a GST, wrapped as it was in Hewson's Fightback package, to win the 1993 election.

'Keating was furious when he couldn't get it through. And I, from opposition, supported it,' says Howard. 'And then he turns around and attacks Hewson and wins the election.'

You write in *The Menzies Era* about Hawke's decision not to debate you in the '87 election, arguing that 'an indulgent media accepted the superficial excuse that he'd already debated me many times in Parliament'. Do you believe he was indulged by the press?

'He was massively indulged,' says Howard. 'And the fact that when Hawke embraced policies that we'd been advocating and they'd previously attacked, they didn't seem to lose any paint for their hypocrisy. But that [the '87 debate] was a very good example. For years, the media had quite rightly argued that we should be debating, and the first debate was in 1984 and Peacock did very well against Hawke in that debate. It was for that reason that Hawke didn't want to debate me. Those debates, the atmospherics of them, always favour the challenger.

'People's assumption is because somebody's already prime minister he's going to wipe the floor with his opponent. And when you inevitably don't wipe the floor, because nobody ever wipes the floor with his opponent in these circumstances, people think, "Oh, that opposition leader is quite good, isn't he?"'

How did you feel when Hawke convinced John Singleton to handle the ALP's '87 campaign?

'Well, I remember Whingeing Wendy.' Which, says Howard, 'was a legitimate campaign ploy. I don't bear any grudges about something like that. I frankly don't bear many grudges about anything. What's the point?'

In his memoirs, Hawke describes you thus: 'Unlike Andrew Peacock, who was more the amiable dilettante, Howard was a hard-working, fully professional politician.' Was there always a mutual respect?

'It's grown stronger in more recent years,' says Howard. 'But Bob Hawke was somebody who had his eyes on the main prize from a very early stage and therefore he analysed his opponents very carefully.'

How will Hawke's government be remembered?

'It'll be seen as the most competent Labor government since World War II ... Hawke is the best Labor prime minister Australia's had. I underline the word Labor.'

In a list of prime ministers since Federation where does Hawke rank?

'It goes without saying that I don't rate him as high as somebody like Menzies.'

Can we get a little more precise?

'It's pretty precise, isn't it? To say he's the best Labor prime minister?'

Would you regard Hawke as among the top five best Australian prime ministers ever?

'That's my opinion,' says Howard, on the cusp of boil. 'Don't press me any further.'

If we're not going to compare left with right, how about Labor v. Labor. Who was the superior prime minister, Hawke or Keating?

'Oh,' says Howard, 'Hawke was a *much better* prime minister.'

— CHAPTER 15 —

BOB TURNS
EIGHTY-SEVEN

THE READER WILL NOT BE SHOCKED TO LEARN THAT Hawke isn't a man to let a birthday swing past without some bawdy fun. While others cower from the anniversary, Hawke announces and flaunts his age.

Let's catalogue recent milestones.

The seventieth, 1999. In the games room, which is located on level one of Hawke's four-level house, the full-sized billiard table is pushed out of the way and ice statues of a nude woman and man are filled with white wine. The woman dispenses wine from her breasts, the man from his penis. One notable guest delights partygoers when she declines a glass and instead presses her mouth to the male's member to receive her wine.

A band plays. Terrific speeches are made. John Singleton arrives late and, slightly boozed, announces his gift of a quarter-share in the soon-to-be-champion yearling Belle du Jour.

The eightieth, 2009. Bennelong restaurant at Sydney Opera House is festooned with ALP greats, including Paul Keating and Kim Beazley. Current Labor prime minister Kevin Rudd also attends, despite an earlier missive from his office to say that he won't. Hawke, who doesn't usually dance, surprises guests when he waltzes Blanche around the room, something he practised two weeks for.

The crowd is thrilled when burlesque performer Ms Gypsy Wood, whose appearance has been arranged by naughty Louis and Blanche, steps onto the stage wearing an oversized John Howard mask and performs a striptease to 'God Save the Queen' and, later, 'Sorry Seems to Be the Hardest Word'.

Not everyone is pleased. The right-wing columnist Andrew Bolt responds by drawing a parallel with the *Footy Show* host Sam Newman, who'd been 'hounded off air' after he affixed a female sportswriter's head onto a bikini-clad mannequin.

John Howard took the performance in good humour.

'I was certainly not offended,' Mr Howard told the *Sydney Morning Herald*. 'It was very gracious of Bob to invite me to his party, and I'm glad to know that after two years I still bug the Labor Party.'

Eight years later, on birthday eighty-seven, Hawke wakes at 7.30, several hours earlier than usual, and is driven to Sydney University, where he is presented with an honorary doctorate.

The degree is awarded in recognition of his government's environmental agenda, and its profound and politically brave economic reforms, as well as significant achievements such as the reintroduction of Medicare.

The uni's chancellor, Belinda Hutchinson, describes Hawke as a 'truly great Australian whose contribution to our nation has been extraordinary and indeed genuinely legendary'.

Hawke uses the occasion to push his Australia-as-world's-nuclear-repository idea: 'We now have the capacity either, on the one hand, to improve the standards and quality of life of all of mankind or, on the other, to destroy life as we know it. Let me assure you,' he says, 'that's not the fanciful imaginations of an old man. The fact of global warming will not go away whether you are president elect of the United States or a humble citizen of Australia.'

Prior to Hawke, prior to the chancellor, the leader of the opposition, Bill Shorten – who, unlike Hawke, is hardly five-feet-seven of pure heaven – loosens up and delivers an excellent speech on the man whose shadow he is forever caught in.

It's a tremendous privilege to say a few words today in honour of a Labor legend.

And, Bob, I must begin with two very important words: Happy birthday.

Whenever I go for a jog around Canberra, I run past the statues of three prime ministers. The pace I'm moving at usually gives me time to study them in detail.

On the path between the old boarding houses of Barton and old Parliament House, Ben Chifley and John Curtin walk side by side. It's a quiet moment in a busy day. Two friends swapping a story, sharing a laugh. Two giants, sharing the burden of winning a war, securing a peace, building a society worthy of the sacrifice of so many Australians.

Further down, on the shores of the lake he inaugurated, Robert Menzies walks alone. Prime minister before Curtin, and then again after Chifley. There's a smile on his face, a glint in his eye. It's the expression of a man who has known success – and knows it will come again.

And so, friends, as we gather to celebrate an eighty-seventh birthday and an honorary doctorate, I ask myself – how would a sculptor capture Bob Hawke? Microphone or megaphone in one hand, the other moving in time with his words – rallying, inspiring and delighting a crowd. Perhaps with head cocked, one hand grasping his earlobe, listening respectfully to an Aboriginal elder, a captain of industry, an American president or a local parent out doing their shopping. Or maybe in the stands at Moonee Valley, creased and folded form guide in hand, ticking off another winner – or not. Or in that jacket, mouth open with laughter, dodging the champagne, giving his prime ministerial blessing to a good old-fashioned sickie.

Whatever pose they opted for, the statue could never be tucked away in a corner of the capital. It would have to be out among the Australian people. The people with whom he shared a connection never seen before in Australian politics. The people whose wisdom he trusted – and whose support he secured more often than any other Labor leader. The Australian people loved Bob Hawke because they could tell he loved them. Australians know he still loves them – and they still love him.

And, friends, the more I thought about that sculpture, the more I realised no matter how lifelike the bronze, no matter how skilled the hands that shape it, no artist can surpass the monuments Bob has already built.

If you want to see a tribute to Bob Hawke, look around you.

This world-class university, where places are earned on merit – not purchased by privilege.

An Australia where kids from working-class families finish school. Less than three in ten kids did that when Bob came to office – eight in ten when he left.

A modern, outward-looking, competitive economy, where working- and middle-class people are rewarded for their efforts. A system built on the idea that growth is stronger when it is shared, when wages and living standards rise – and a strong safety net catches those who fall on hard times.

A country where tourists and locals alike share the

wonders of the Daintree or ride the rapids of the Franklin.

An Australia at home in Asia, a voice heard and respected in the councils of the world. A country that steps up and plays its part – keeping peace in the Middle East, keeping Antarctica safe for science.

And if you want to see a monument to Bob Hawke, open your wallet or your purse or your bag and look at your Medicare card: a green-and-gold promise that the health of any Australian matters to all Australians. He built Medicare – and last election, he campaigned with us to save it.

So many of those achievements have earned the ultimate compliment from Bob's political opponents – they now pretend to have supported them all along.

As prime minister, consensus was Bob's watchword. But that didn't mean taking the soft option, the low road, the path of least resistance. It didn't mean floating thought bubbles in the morning and popping them in the afternoon. Or blinking and backtracking at the first sign of resistance. Bob – and the brilliant cabinet he chaired so assuredly – built consensus. They understood that consensus meant leading and persuading – not surrender, retreat and division.

Friends, history can be the most brutal judge. But it is also the most compelling. As president of the ACTU, Bob was the champion of unpopular causes.

- The right of unions to organise and bargain.
- Opposing French nuclear testing in the Pacific.
- Opposing the war in Vietnam.
- Opposing apartheid – and defending Nelson Mandela, when conservatives were branding him a terrorist.

As prime minister, he was a force for consensus – but on Labor terms.

Bob was the great unifier – but he was also a great separator. He opposed trickle-down economics – the Reaganite, Thatcherite fashion of the times – now back in vogue.

In Australian history, in Australian politics, there was B.H. and A.H. Before Hawke – and After Hawke.

After Hawke, we were a different country. A kinder, better country.

He worked with Keating and Kelty to negotiate a national [Prices and Incomes] Accord.

He swiftly and decisively implemented Medicare.

He worked sensitively and with humility to engage with Asia. Not lecturing from the podium of Australia but constantly working in hundreds of meetings to build relationships with the region.

Of course, Bob Hawke is special. There will never be another Hawke government – because there will only ever be one Bob Hawke.

Very rarely, in the world, are countries defined by a leader's time in power. Before FDR – and after FDR. Before Lee Kuan Yew – and after Lee Kuan Yew.

It's rare to say you changed a country and left it different. It's even more rare to say you changed it for the better. Kinder, more open, more confident. Deakin did it. Curtin and Chifley did it. Gough did it. And so did Bob.

That's Dr Robert James Lee Hawke.

That's who we celebrate today.

Bob – that is your place in history.

— CHAPTER 16 —

THE STEPSON

L OUIS PRATT, THE ONLY CHILD OF BLANCHE D'ALPUGET and Tony Pratt, was conceived in Jakarta, born in Kuala Lumpur and raised in Canberra's 'steamroller of banality and domesticity,' as his mother describes it.

Louis was four when Hawke and his mother became lovers, six when she was dumped by Hawke and fourteen when she left the family home for good and moved to Sydney. Tony had insisted that, as she was the one breaking up the marriage, she could not take Louis to live with her.

'I remember this sense of sadness that I didn't know why my mum wasn't at the house,' says Louis. There was a brief period when Blanche and Tony attempted a reconciliation. 'But it was a wounded relationship.'

Blanche and Louis had a spectacular falling-out.

'We both have fiery tempers and during the argument a tea towel actually burst into flame. Our relationship broke down completely,' says Blanche. 'Louis said he'd never speak to me again. I was devastated, and there were very few people I could or would confide in, because to do so my affair with Bob could come out. One person I did tell was Susan Ryan. I used to cry on her shoulder about Louis. "He'll come back," she'd say. We had some meetings, but they were difficult . . . Louis and I had a rapprochement when he was sixteen. An American friend who saw us together said, "He loves you madly."'

'You know, I take marriage very seriously,' says Louis. 'Going through a divorce as a child at that age, it fucks you up a bit. You somehow think it's your fault or you were involved in it. Because that's your world, your family. And then when it all starts to fall apart, you're like, "What have I done? Have I done something?"'

Louis is forty-four years old now and has inherited the miraculous genes of his mother and grandmother. He hovers a little over six feet, has wide blue eyes, pale and mostly unlined skin and a relatively stubborn carpet of dark red curls constrained by a small-brimmed hat perched kippah-like on his crown.

He wears the uniform of the inner-city creative: a slim-fitting, scoop-neck white T-shirt, black jeans and work boots. A scarf loosely circles his neck. Call him thirty and you'll get fewer raised eyebrows than the reveal of his actual vintage.

Louis survived the divorce, as children mostly do, and flourished. He completed three degrees: a BA in graphic design, a BA in visual arts (first-class honours) and a Masters of Fine Arts, majoring in new technology. He was a lecturer at Sydney's College of Fine Arts from 2003–2015, teaching metal casting, 3D animation, 3D printing and using technology to make art. Now, with commissions piling up for his 3D-printed sculptures, and with his work bought for private collections in Australia, Switzerland, China, Germany, England and America, Louis has become that rarest of birds, the self-sufficient artist.

The first time I wanted to interview Louis he was busy with a sculpture for the Bendigo hospital, a $300,000, six-tonne work called *Alchemy*.

Could I call back in a few weeks? A month?

Three months later, the work is about to be installed in the hospital's therapeutic garden. Louis is leaving for Bendigo the following day, but I ask if I can swing by and inspect his art at his studio in Marrickville, in Sydney's inner west.

The first item to draw the visitor's gaze is the almost-life-sized sculpture of a couple locked in a carnal embrace. The man, whom we presume to be nude, angles his pelvis upwards. The woman completes the docking sequence by tilting her pubis downwards. The scene is made surreal by heads of polygon planes and bodies of sharp angles. The lovers are wrapped in gold flake and mounted on a mirrored plinth. Louis thinks he'll call the work *Corrupt File* because of his 'fascination with the human body and also this concept of personal data and pornography and the dehumanising nature of both,' he says.

To create the lifelike forms, Louis either buys data or scans a model or a friend. He uses a hired structured light scanner and then manipulates and reduces the data to create the effect he seeks. The 3D printers he owns and maintains himself.

Beside *Corrupt File* is a gold apple with a blackened core, the size of a baby hippopotamus. It's one of a prize-winning, politically motivated series about coal and energy that 'draws upon the biblical motif of the apple, of original sin, that there *are* consequences of using coal,' he says. 'Of course we needed at a certain stage to burn coal to generate electricity to generate technology to get where we are. But there are consequences.'

The large apple you can buy for $6666, smaller versions for $666.

'Making a pact with the devil,' he says.

Louis keeps regular enough hours at the studio and has just bought a small apartment in nearby Newtown. Not that he's going to be dragging his bags into the city anytime soon.

He expects he'll be living for a while yet in the harbourfront boatshed he's called home since 2009, when the lease on a sprawling house he shared with three friends in the beachside suburb of Bronte ended and the group couldn't find a joint to fit them all in. If you're in a jam, come and throw your gear in the boatshed, Blanche suggested. It wasn't a difficult sell. The small wooden structure has a loft-bed built into its vaulted roof, a bathroom and a jetty in front where he and Bob can snatch the occasional fish.

Bob is the stepfather Louis didn't eyeball up close until he was twenty-three, just before his mother's 1995 wedding at the Ritz in Double Bay. The first Louis knew of the lovers going public in 1994 was when he saw it on the news while holidaying in Port Douglas.

When they did meet, Hawke told him straight up, 'I just want you to know I think of you as my own son.'

'He was very open and generous from day one,' says Louis.

The living arrangement suits Hawke and Blanche as much as it does Louis. In return for a rent-free existence in his little perch on the water, Louis will cook dinner, buy the shiraz blends Hawke prefers and nail any odd jobs. More importantly, given Hawke's inquisitive intelligence and his need to comprehend the shifting nature of work and living, Louis has become Hawke's connection to the world of new technologies.

'I'm very tech-savvy. I use a lot of software and machines. We talk about automation, artificial intelligence, technological singularity [the hypothesis that AI will lead to unimagined consequences] and how it all works today. How it's changing the face of the job market,' he says. 'It's probably what has kept wages quite flat. All around the world is a flattening of wage growth. Lots of jobs are disappearing.'

Wage growth and a shifting labour market. Oh, tell me that wouldn't be right up Hawke's alley . . .

'Well, yeah,' says Louis, 'because he saw that the best way for a society to improve was to get jobs for everyone and raise the minimum wage. If you raise the minimum wage you are just putting more money back into the economy. All these people think you have to screw down the minimum wage because it's going to hurt business. It's not true because you are going to get rid of customers who have the money to pay for things.'

Wait until jobs are increasingly automated, says Louis. 'Things are going to be problematic if we create this whole useless class of people. What's a truck driver going do when trucks are robot-driven? And it's going to happen soon.'

Louis tells me that Hawke has set up a research project into the effect of artificial intelligence, how it will shape the job market and how society can negotiate it.

'You don't know its capabilities or even its ethics,' he says. 'Maybe it has profiles in there, such as no human can be harmed, but maybe to save the human race from itself it thinks, *I have to kill three million people to do it*. Bob really wanted to get his head around AI so I dug up some Harvard papers on the decimation of the workforce. They're saying that in the next twenty years, 41 per cent of jobs in America are going to be under threat.'

Until Hawke's feet gave out and the one-drink-a-night-rule came into effect ('That's Mum putting the fun squeeze on him,' he says), Louis and his old pal would have boozy nights wiping out whole bottles of Scotch and playing snooker.

'We would carry on, a lot of yelling. He's very funny,' says Louis.

These days they watch the golf and bet on putts. Louis digs their time together but he misses the ambulatory Hawke.

'It's an unfortunate thing to happen, because once you stop walking there's so many things you don't do. And then you become more sedentary and so it exacerbates the original problem. When they get to that age, they're sort of . . . [long pause] . . . *drifting* away from you. It's sad. And I can see my mum – you know how vital she is and she's really fit. So it's a problem.'

Louis acts as an unofficial minder for his stepdad at functions. He'll hang in the background, keeping an eye on Hawke, making sure he's okay.

'I know him so well I know if something isn't right,' he says.

How did you feel when the press sunk the boot into Hawke and Blanche?

'She really was the scarlet woman,' says Louis. 'I remember Mum saying she lived in a hotel for a while trying to hide away from it all. Falling in love and committing was always a risk. And it affected Mum more than Bob. Hazel had a special place in the Australian psyche, and they didn't want to see her being treated badly.'

But, he says, Hawke and Blanche 'offer an inspiration to lots of people as they get older. That it is possible to fall in love. And when they were just getting married Mum was like a teenager again.'

Hawke at eighty-seven?

Louis describes him as a pacifist, still driven by a sense that what matters, above everything, is the Brotherhood of Man.

'He has a love of helping people. He thinks of other people first and you can see that was what drove him as a politician. It's just really the generosity of his sprit. The continual fight for Australians. Or anyone. It's rare that you meet someone that's happy to get out there and fight for another person – and then do it phenomenally well.'

Do you regard Hawke as a friend or a father figure?

'A friend, because I was brought up by my dad and we met as adults,' Louis says.

But: 'I love him like a father.'

— CHAPTER 17 —

COL CUNNINGHAM

C OLIN CUNNINGHAM, HAWKE'S PAL SINCE 1972 – HIS dearest, if such things can be definitively catalogued – doesn't exactly *leap* at my request for an interview.

Col tells me he's said everything that he's ever likely to say about his mate in the *Australian Story* episode that aired in 2014 and, anyway, he's in Melbourne and I'm in Sydney.

I tell him I'll jump on a bird any day that suits.

'Nah, nah, nah, don't bother coming down. There's nuthin' left to say,' Col barks down his ancient plastic phone.

But...

... since it's coming up to his eighty-fifth birthday and he plans to be in Sydney, maybe we could have a little chinwag then.

Doesn't like the rain, though. If it rains, he's not coming.

Col says that before Bobby swapped his Sandringham digs for Kirribilli House in Sydney, he'd come home from some trip or another, and say, 'Col, we come up here and we get drowned every time. It's the biggest con ever been pulled on man, telling us about the weather up here.' Col won't have it either.

It rains.

Hawke asks me, 'Have you interviewed Col yet?'

'We're negotiating. About the weather.'

Hawke laughs.

Another phone call. Col comes around.

Two weeks later, on a sparkling thirty-one-degree autumn day in Melbourne (Sydney is soaking in its wettest March since Fraser had the wheel), I meet Col at the William Angliss cooking school on La Trobe street, right there in the heart of the city.

'It's a Herculean task to write another silly fucking book about Bob Hawke,' he says, leading me through the rabbit warren of training kitchens, past the student café and into a mezzanine level with four-metre-high floor-to-ceiling windows and a low-slung black couch.

As for Col, even this late in the game he looks like he's about to tap-dance straight onto centre court at Kooyong or swing a stick at Royal Melbourne. He wears Nike trainers, blue-and-green madras shorts and a pink Yonex polo shirt, with a cap pulled low across his forehead and a backpack swinging off one shoulder. Only slightly bent with age, I estimate the octogenarian to measure a little under six feet. His skin has been belted by the sun, as is typical for a lifetime tennis player and golfer. A scabby red island adrift on a sea of pink defines his right temple. Various other pieces of skin threaten their moorings, too. I promise myself I'll be more diligent with sunscreen on my own face. But, whatever. Not bad for a digger heading towards ninety.

'Come here much?' I say.

'Two or three times a week for the last thirty years,' he says.

Col places his backpack on the floor and empties the contents, one by one.

First, a packet of biscuits.

'Ah, well, I like a bickie.'

Then plums.

'Blood plums, you like those?'

Oh, I do!

Pears.

'Yeah, yeah, I like my pears.'

Then an old envelope with six photos inside. We see Hawke and Col at the Sandown Park races in 1973; Col and his wife Gloria with Bob and Hazel at the Lodge for Hawke's sixtieth birthday; a photo that snatches the view of Sailors Bay from Hawke's joint in Northbridge; and three shots of Hawke playing golf in 2009.

'Good swing,' I say.

'He thinks it is.'

What's Hawke like as a golfer?

'Oh, he used to be alright. He's stuffed now. He told me, "I'm good as gold myself but I just can't walk. He sees me playing and says, "How old are you? Eighty-five? *Jesus!*"'

I tell Col I've just had an email from Blanche telling me the nerves in Hawke's feet have switched back on and he's starting to get a little feeling back.

'Is he? *Shit!* That's a result.'

So let's get to know Col.

Are you a bookie?

'Punter.'

More than a punter. Col grew up in the slums of Melbourne, the son of a cab driver, and left school in grade seven to work the stables for the city's leading horse trainer and jockey, Fred Hoysted. Five in the morning until six every night. Thirty bob a week.

The kid learned to play golf. Became a bit of a hotshot and won five premierships at the Long Island Country Club in Frankston, a course owned by bookies and publicans back in the days when 'if you didn't have blue blood in your veins they didn't fucken want ya. So they bought their own course.' Col used to play the bookies for cash, saw how lucrative their businesses were and ended up working the bag for them at the races.

'In those days, the bookies had *millions,*' he recalls. 'If they went to the races and didn't win five or six or seven thousand pound, when you could buy a house for around three thousand, they'd pull the, "Oh gee, I had a bad day, I only won three thousand!' That was their mentality, you know? People after the war, soldiers, pouring money into the bags, you know? So I went and worked for them.'

And then, says Col, 'I ran into Bobby.'

The story is well-known, but he'll tell it anyway, since I'm here and all. The Polish-born property developer and pub owner Eddie Kornhauser liked a good tip – and Col had the mail, as they say.

'I knew what I was doing,' says Col. 'And I was at the Caulfield Cup one year and Eddie, who was a big, tall Jewish man – usually the Jews are quite small, but Eddie stood out – he said, "Colin! Col! Meet a friend of mine. Bob Hawke, this is Col Cunningham. He's a friend of Roy Higgins. Col plays golf with Roy."'

Roy Higgins. Australia's leading jockey. Won the Melbourne Cup twice. A couple of Cox Plates. Hawke was thrilled at the chance to orbit the little man.

'So Bob says, "Alright, come and have a drink." And so we went and had a drink and that was that. He said, "I'd like to have a game of golf with ya," and I said, "Well, give Gloria a ring, here's my number." He rung on the Monday and I got Roy to come along at the Victoria Golf Club and we went from there.'

Now let's examine the public profile of ACTU president Hawke in 1972. He travelled in a chauffeur-driven Ford LTD limo that had been fitted out with a desk in the back seat so he could work:

> [He] was treated like a grandee. Crowds fawned upon him;
> mobs of nouveaux riches rowdies attached themselves to him
> as cheer squads . . . Recognised wherever he went, Hawke
> moved in an aura of power. Foreign dignitaries who visited
> Australia wanted to meet him: an official of the American
> Embassy commented, 'We had to make a cut-off point of
> seniority. For those below the line we would not even consider
> trying to arrange an appointment with Bob.'

In the case of Col, it was a switcheroo; Hawke latched onto Col.

'Well, I suited Bob,' says Col. 'Bob wanted to play golf. Col liked to play golf. Bob wanted to play tennis. Col played tennis. We'd play, come back to my house, play snooker and drink beer. And I wasn't politically motivated. I was a Labor person, but with the politicians they found it hard to have good friends 'cause it's a nasty business, you know? With me, we got along well. As I say, we hit it off. Everything I liked, *he liked*!'

One of Col's many impressive traits was his ability to befriend sports stars. He had Roy Higgins in his pocket, the golfer Jack Newton, the tennis player Lew Hoad, Davis Cup captain Neale Fraser, boxer Lionel Rose and cricket's greatest all-rounder, Garry Sobers.

Was it an experience to drink with Hawke in those early days prior to his shift into politics?

'He wasn't Nice Bob all the time, you know. He'd carry on a bit. He was a heavy drinker in the early days, Bob. Bad-tempered and all that. He was alright when he was sober but when he was drunk he was a bit different. Do some silly things.'

What sort of silly things?

Col snorts a laugh. 'Look, I can't say a lot of things. I mean, I *could* tell a lot of things, but I don't. And that's one of the reasons why we're still friends. Whatever I saw, and whatever he told me, remained with me. I forgot about [it], you know? As I say, I could write a bestseller. But anyhow . . . '

Tell me about Hawke's capacity to drink, I prompt.

'They say that beer destroys all your things in the brain. Well, he disproves that because he's still got his marbles. He should be a raving lunatic if that was true.'

Were you surprised when he gave up the booze?

'Oh, well, look, he had to. It was just going to be a wasted life. I drove him home one night and Fraser was PM at the time and the country was in disarray. Strikes and so on. And he was hated, Malcolm Fraser. Later he mended his ways, but at that time, he was bad for the average person. And I said to Bob that everyone was looking for [him] to do something. Even though it was ACTU days and he wasn't prime minister, they were looking for . . . him. I said, "You've just got to, Bob. There's too many people depending on ya."'

How did he respond?

'Oh, well, he was rolling drunk at the time.'

Col laughs, and moves on to a story about Hawke and his obsession with the SMOP Tote Buster, an electronic device for picking winners at the horses. Once, the pair flew to Perth together and Hawke spent the five-hour flight with the little device propped on his lap, the machine's paper roll furiously printing predictions for the following day's races.

'He was doing alright for a while,' says Col. 'It was spitting out a few winners. Hazel was telling Gloria that Bob would get into bed at night and pull the bloody thing out. Because, you know, he only sleeps four hours a night. And it drove Hazel bloody mad. The bloody noise! He's up playing with the bloody thing all night!'

Was Bob a good punter?

'He wasn't hopeless. He knew what he was doing at the time. A bit of help doesn't hurt. Bob got matey with Ray Guy on the

Gold Coast and he'd ring Bob up and say, "This has got a good chance, Bob. It's thirty-three-to-one." *Win!* Oh, he was marvellous. Bob got a lot of money out of Ray Guy.'

Would he have a good swing with his bets?

'He'd get up a bit. He'd have fifty or a hundred on something if he liked it. He bet up big when his horse won the [Golden] Slipper. But that's because Singo did it all [betting $100,000 of the syndicate's money at ten-to-one]. They shit themselves! Him and Blanche went home and put their heads under the pillow!'

Oh, how Col laughs at that.

Have you always been close friends? Any fallings-out?

'No! Never had a stink. Nuh. Nuh. *Nuh.* We've never even had harsh words, Bob and I. I think he really liked me. Well, I really liked him. I think he's terrific! Old Bobby. I love him.'

What do you like about Hawke?

'Look, he's just a nice person, yeah? Although he was the wrong one to get accolades of Man of the Year.'

The Victorian Father of the Year in '71?

'Yeah, that was all bullshit. That was stupid. Because he wasn't the father of the year. Everyone knows that. [But] he's honest. He doesn't tell lies. And that's the reason we got on alright. There's no telling fibs and all that bullshit. Speak the truth and if you don't like it, well, that's that.'

On the Wednesday night before Hawke was rolled by Keating on 19 December 1991, Hawke rang Col.

'How are ya?' asked Col.

'I'm alright,' said Hawke, 'but I'm gone. They've got the votes on me.'

'Do you want me to come up?' said Col.

'Yeah, I'd like you to,' replied the beaten leader.

Col jumped on a plane on the morning of Keating's successful challenge and spent the day, and the next night, with the

Hawkes. He remembers waking up early the day after the challenge, going into the main bedroom, and Hawke and Hazel are sitting there and Hawke says, 'What am I going to do now?'

When Hawke got the keys to John Singleton's Birchgrove mansion shortly afterwards, Col and Gloria went to stay there, too.

'They had no other friends, really – he didn't anyhow,' says Col. 'But Birchgrove was good. Taught him to do things for himself. He didn't know what money was! He'd go to a shop and he'd pull out some money and he'd look at it and wouldn't know what to do with it. He hadn't been in that situation for quite a while.'

Those weeks at Birchgrove must be the most precious memories, I suggest.

'Awwww, no, not really, no,' says Col. 'He'd got thrown out. It wasn't much fun in there.'

Was he pissed off?

'He's pretty realistic. He knew days before – weeks before, probably – that the game was up. If he'd done a couple of deals on the side, he would've still been there. He didn't want [Graham] Richardson to get the post as the transport and communications minister and he lost out. If Richo had got the job, he'd have rolled Keating! [Bob] wouldn't go against his principles and it cost him his job.'

When the 1990–91 cabinet papers were released after their quarter-of-a-century embargo, Hawke told the State Library of NSW, 'I really settled my fate soon after the election in 1990. Those of you who have read the story will read that I refused to give Graham Richardson the transport and communications portfolio, something which he'd set his heart on. The background to that was that my dear friend Peter Abeles had told me something concerning Graham which in my judgement precluded him properly being in that position.

'Because I still have a great deal of affection for Graham Richardson and because he's in very bad shape, I'm not going to go to that issue because it would be hurtful for him. But I knew once I made that decision to refuse him what he wanted that he would turn his support and his very, very considerable influence with the New South Wales Right to Paul, and that's what he did.'

Richo responded by saying it was either 'amnesia or malice' that drove Hawke's comments.

Either way, Richo switched sides and Hawke was out. And it gave Hawke the opening to eventually formalise his affair.

When did you first find out about Blanche?

'Awwww . . .'

Long pause.

'I wouldn't want to say. I don't want to say . . . no . . . *no*.'

Did Hawke talk to you about Blanche?

'No, he didn't. Bob keeps things to himself; I didn't enquire. You do your business, I'll do mine and Bob's your uncle.'

Did he ever seek your advice?

'Why would he want my advice? He's smart enough without me, Bobby! On a golf course or a race track he might.'

Describe your current relationship with Hawke.

'He's been hard to talk to on the phone since he's been deaf. *What did you say?* Screaming and yelling, oh geez. So, to be honest, I just speak to [Hawke's secretary] Jill. *Look, I want to do this, tell him.*'

Col had told Jill he'd be in Sydney for his eighty-fifth, but it didn't happen because of a poor weather forecast. When Col didn't show, Jill called and asked where he was.

'Getting off a bus in Port Melbourne.'

'But I arranged a dinner for you and Bob,' said Jill.

'Well, Jill, I'm not coming up.'

Col leaps to his feet, holds an imaginary golf stick and starts to swing at equally imaginary balls.

'And I'm hitting balls about three o'clock, and I've got the phone down there on the ground, it rings, I pick up and . . .'

Col mimics Hawke's deep basso. *'HAPPY BIRTHDAY TO YOU! HAPPY BIRTHDAY TO YOU! HAPPY BIRTHDAY TO YOOOOOOOOOOU, HAPPY BIRTHDAY TO YOU!'*

'It took him three minutes to get through it,' says Col. 'I'm on the green and everyone could hear it. Oh yeah, he's got a voice on him.'

A student chef on an upper level drops a pepper grinder into the void.

'You want me to throw it back?' hollers Col. 'Jesus! Where are ya?'

A spotty teen chef waves a hand. Col loops the grinder in an arc that lands square in her meaty palm.

'Good shot,' she says.

'Good on ya!' Col waves.

What do you think Hawke has given you as a friend?

'We've just enjoyed our relationship. I helped his kids open doors when they were the scatterbrained type. Ros [Bob's daughter] – I helped him with that. And as soon as he became prime minister, my son John was in the army and he was up in Sydney and I said, "Go and have a look at Kirribilli House, he's over there." So I rung up Bob and he said, no worries, and John went over and had a look around. When he was away, I'd go to Kirribilli and invite friends over there for dinner. Not bad was it?'

What's the kindest thing Hawke's ever done for you?

'I don't know if he's done any kind things, has he? Paid for me to go to Japan [to check out horse studs]. I've helped him a lot. There were a few sticky moments in the seventies when he needed looking after. Deep down he probably appreciates it. I hope.'

Has he changed as a man over the years?

'Changed? He's stuffed now, isn't he. He's slow, poor bastard. I rung him up when he was sick, probably eighteen months ago, I said, "What's wrong with ya?" He said, "Colin, I've got old."'

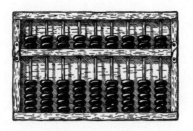

— CHAPTER 18 —

'HOU KE' GOES
TO CHINA

B OB HAWKE'S FRIEND AND GENERAL SECRETARY OF THE Communist Party of China Zhao Ziyang had been in the job for eighteen months, when People's Liberation Army units began their 4 am sweep of pro-democracy demonstrators in Beijing's Tiananmen Square.

The atrocities quickly mounted. Diplomatic cables from the Canadian embassy in Beijing back to Ottawa reported:

> An old woman knelt in front of soldiers pleading for students; soldiers killed her.
> A boy was seen trying to escape holding a woman with a two-year-old child in a stroller, and was run over by a tank.
> The tank turned around and mashed them up.
> Soldiers fired machine guns until the ammo ran out.

The cables also mentioned unconfirmed reports of soldiers' corpses found garrotted in canals.

> The country is now being controlled by a group of vicious

elderly generals and the government is run by people who will blindly follow their orders. The situation looks grim at best.

The demonstrations had begun six weeks earlier when another of Hawke's good friends, the popular reformist Hu Yaobang, had died suddenly of a heart attack.

Little Hu, 'a tiny, excitable extrovert', says Hawke, represented the liberal heart of the Communist Party. He wasn't just about easing China away from orthodox Marxism and into a free-market economy (which even the old generals acknowledged had to happen); he wanted to squeeze corruption from the highest levels of office and loosen the binds on public criticism of the party. A hero to progressives and students; a gadfly to the hard-liners.

In December 1986 and through the middle of January 1987, students in seventeen cities across China protested the lack of political reform. Hu, then the Communist Party's general secretary, did little to quash the demonstrations.

Perceived by party leader Deng Xiaoping as too bourgeois – and possibly as punishment for revealing state secrets in his conversations with Hawke ('He didn't tell me any state secrets,' says Hawke) – Hu was forced to resign in 1987 and was replaced by Zhao Ziyang.

On state television, a statement confected by the party was read, explaining that Hu had resigned after making 'a self-criticism of his mistakes on major issues of political principles in violation of the party's principle of collective leadership'.

Hu's death in April created the spark among students to start his reformist program. One hundred thousand students marched on his state funeral in Tiananmen Square. The protests continued through May and into June.

When cables from the Australian embassy in Beijing landed on his desk, graphically describing the bloodshed in Tiananmen

Square, Hawke tearfully announced on television that all Chinese nationals legally in Australia on temporary entry visas would have those visas extended for twelve months, with the right to work as well as financial assistance.

'I was heartbroken and I wept,' says Hawke, who only three years earlier had convinced Zhao of the value of the party allowing Chinese students to study in Australia.

'Before I went on television, I'd just had the communication describing the crushing of some of the students. It was a tragedy. Zhao Ziyang had gone there and offered the woman leader of the students a way out. He told her, if you disperse and go away, we'll look at your concerns. And they wouldn't disperse. I attach a lot of blame to her to for not responding positively to Zhao Ziyang. When I came off [air], the bureaucrats said to me, "Prime Minister, you can't do that." I said, "I've done it. It's done."'

The decision would have dramatic political and social ramifications. Forty-two thousand Chinese students would eventually be granted permanent visas, the total number of Chinese migrants swelling to more than 100,000 after family reunions, resulting in 'the biggest wave of Chinese migration since the gold rush of the 1850s'.

In 2003, Monash University's director for Population and Urban Research, Dr Bob Birrell, said, 'Whatever way you look at it, it's a massive transformation of Sydney, and Sydney is almost a third overseas-born now, and a third of that third are Asian.'

Foreign fee-paying students are now a $19 billion industry, Australia's third-biggest export after coal and iron ore.

Cabinet papers from 1989 reveal that Minister for Immigration Robert Ray told his colleagues that allowing 16,000 Chinese into Australia would smash the yearly refugee intake of 14,000. Ray feared the decision would give impetus to other marginalised groups to seek similar visa extensions.

'The Kurds, Afghans and Lebanese have already reacted with hostility,' Ray told cabinet.

For Hawke, China was different to the quagmire of the Middle East, with its perennial wars and ancient feuds. Like Whitlam and Fraser before him, he recognised the importance of not just engaging with but embracing meaningfully the emerging superpower. When he visited China as ACTU leader in 1978, Deng Xiaoping had just become leader of a country with a per capita income of less than US$100 a year.

'Everyone's in Mao suits. There's no advertising. Everyone's on bicycles. Really very primitive,' says Hawke. 'But, you know, I liked the people. I warmed to the Chinese people. It was a very fortunate trip because that was the year that Deng Xiaoping made what I've described as the most important peacetime decision made by any political leader in the world in the twentieth century [to open China to world markets], because it totally transformed China. The decision moved China to a position where it had many successive years of 10 per cent per annum real growth. Nothing like that had ever happened before in the world. It lifted millions of Chinese people out of poverty... [It] just transformed the global economy because it brought the best part of three billion people into the world global market economy.'

The effect of bringing China into world markets wasn't just economic, says Hawke. It smashed the Soviets.

'What happened in China was the most important factor in the collapse of the Soviet Union,' he says. 'When I went up as prime minister, I said to Zhao Ziyang that the Soviets must be very interested in what you're doing. Zhao pretty much said to me, "Every day, hundreds and hundreds of Soviet officials and citizens cross the border. They come and see transformation in the lives of our people. They'd go back and compare it with their sclerotic economy."'

When Hawke visited the Soviet Union in 1987 he told Mikhail Gorbachev, the country's last leader before the Soviet Union was dissolved four years later, that the Chinese had got it right and the Soviets had got it terribly wrong; that economic reform had to happen before any dramatic political shift.

'Socialism and market economy are not incompatible,' as Deng Xiaoping had said.

'The Chinese were concentrating on reforming the economy, knowing that social and political reform would follow that,' says Hawke. 'I said to Gorbachev, "You're concentrating on political reform and your economy is just collapsing." That was a fact. It soon collapsed. So that brought all the hundreds of millions of the Soviet Union and the Soviet empire into the global market. The other factor which is not so often appreciated was India. India had not been a command economy like the Soviets, but it was very much influenced by it. And it was only when the Soviet Union collapsed that it started to move itself towards a more market-oriented economy. So, the best part of three billion people, as a result of that decision in 1978, were brought into that market.'

What was the mood like in 1978? Buoyant, now that the dark days of Mao's Cultural Revolution were behind them?

'Well, there was a bloody great sense of relief that the Gang of Four was gone,' says Hawke, who had refused to visit China until the four party officials who were blamed, and tried, for the worst excesses of the Cultural Revolution were out of the game. 'But it was too early to have any idea of the impact of what Deng Xiaoping's decision would be. One of the decent things Fraser had done was issue an invitation to Zhao Ziyang, the premier, to come to Australia in April 1983. [When the visit took place] I'd just become prime minister and Zhao Ziyang and I hit it off immediately.'

Hawke tells a fine story of having dinner with Zhao and former speaker of the house Billy Snedden.

'I was talking to someone on my left and Ziyang was there and Snedden leaned across him and said, "Prime Minister, I think we should congratulate the premier on his use of a knife and fork." I thought, *Oh shit*. I looked across the table at the Chinese interpreter. She rolled her eyes. I rolled my eyes.'

Was that common behaviour thirty years ago? To be thrilled to see a Chinese man using a knife and fork?

'No, no, no, no. Snedden was just an idiot,' says Hawke. (Four years later, Snedden would famously die of a heart attack between the legs of his son's former lover, who worked in his electoral office. 'It was an adrenalin-filled evening. I'm sure the old man went out happy. Anyone would be proud to die on the job,' said the old cocksmith's son.)

Hawke has said that no other national leader had spent as many hours as he did in direct, intimate discussion with the Chinese leadership. Why were you able to conduct such direct and intimate discussions? I ask. Was it because of your straight-shooting personality?

'Well, it was partly personality. We were no *threat* to them and they needed our great resources, our mineral resources and energy resources, as they were moving towards a highly developed economy. There was quite a natural basis for the relationship.'

As the relationship deepened, Hawke explains, he became a conduit between the USA and China.

'It was recognised that I had developed a closer relationship with the Chinese leadership than any other western leader,' he says. 'The United States believed that China and the Soviet were getting too close together. And so the Chinese asked me to *assure* the American leadership that it was an economic relationship, but that they were at arm's length politically.'

How did the Chinese feel about the Americans?

'They were worried that there was an element within the

United States which was strongly anti-China and pro-Taiwan. But they weren't antagonistic. They wanted to be cooperative.'

In your view, is it madness for the west to rattle its sabre over Taiwan?

'The sensible people in the United States realise that China is a fact of life now. It's the biggest economy in the world and it has an enormous impact on what happens in the world.'

After Tiananmen Square in 1989, Hawke wouldn't visit China again as prime minister.

'Of course, Tiananmen Square ended the close relationship then, and although we [maintained] diplomatic relations, the closeness went. Then, the year after I finished as prime minister, there was a call from the Chinese consul, asking if he could come and see me. He said that he'd been asked by the Chinese government if I would go to China. I said, "Yes, of course I will," because as far as I was concerned I was very sad about what happened but I wanted to look forward to the future. And it's a marvellous indication of just how wise and understanding the Chinese leadership was, because I went up there and went straight to the state guesthouse, and you wait there until you're told the meeting's on. I was summoned to meet Jiang Zemin, who was then the head of China. And I went down and he had about half-a-dozen of his inner cabinet there. I walked in and he got up and walked across and took my hand and he said, "Mr Hawke, there's one thing I want to say to you."

'And, I thought, *Oh shit! What's this?* And he said, "China never forgets its friends. I want you to know that we regard you as one of our best friends." They understood that I'd wept for China and I really did love the Chinese people. And so the relationship resumed then.'

Hawke laughs at the understatement. He's just back from a week in China, his 105th trip to the country. He's popular among the Chinese people because, in Blanche's words, 'they recognised he was non-racist and had benevolent feelings toward their country . . . Over the decades, thanks to many television and newspaper interviews, Hawke became one of the most recognised foreign faces in China and could not walk down a Beijing lane without people shouting "Hou Ke! Hou Ke!" and calling friends to come out of houses to look at him.'

Hawke blazes a $39 Davidoff, visibly thrilled to be out of the suit and tie and into sweats and loafers, back on his terrace awash with spring sun.

Apart from giving speeches, I ask, what business do you conduct in China?

'I represent Australian companies and I represent Chinese companies,' Hawke replies. 'One of the big things I've done in the past year [involves] a Chinese billionaire based in Shanghai – Mr Wu, from the Zhongfu Group. He took me on as an adviser and I negotiated with the Western Australian government over all that Ord River territory, which had never been developed, they're doing a magnificent job up there.' The Zhongfu Group plans to irrigate 13,400 hectares at a cost of $700 million. In return for the work, the company pays the state government one dollar per year rent.

What's it like when you negotiate with an Australian premier? Do they tremble at the thought of trying to outmanoeuvre the famous ACTU gunslinger? The man who convinced Australians to re-elect him at the height of the country's worst-ever recession?

'Ha! I don't know about that. I get on with all governments, whether they're Labor or not. I got on well in negotiations with Barnett, the Western Australian Liberal premier, who was very good.'

What are the key elements of strong negotiation?

'You've got to be direct and truthful and tell it as it is. Don't overblow it. You want people to know that they can trust you and your client.'

Where will China be in twenty years?

'It *will be* the number one [world] power.'

Can you describe what China will look like socially in twenty years?

'China's an infinitely freer and more liberal country now than it was in 1978. That will go on. I mean, this president, he's a pretty tough guy. He's very seriously anti-corruption, and that's very big; [it's] very important they absolutely get that under control. And they've shown a capacity to adapt to changing economic circumstances, and I think they'll continue to do that. They'll never go back to 10 per cent per annum real growth, but they have a bit over 6 per cent, which most countries would kill for.'

Is there any reason for Australians, or the west, to be concerned about China's rise? It's obviously an opportunity, but is it also a threat?

'No, I don't think it's a threat. The absolute condition of this period of growth has been reasonable stability. It's no accident that this period of the Chinese economic revolution from the late 1970s has coincided with the most peaceful period in Asia's history.'

What do Sino-Japanese relations look like now?

'Tense.' Hawke pauses. 'The Chinese will never forget the Second World War and there's the [contested Senkaku] islands. But they will cope. I mean, the important relationship is America.'

How will the decline of America and the rise of China affect Australia?

'The American relationship will always remain important, but China's our major trading partner and has been for some time now. That's the important factor. You're not going to just willingly and easily do things which are going to disturb that economic relationship.'

Do you believe the Chinese Communist Party, even now, is the best government for China?

'Let me put it this way,' says Hawke. 'I believe if you were to have a free election in China now, the Communist Party would win because the Chinese people are very proud of what's been accomplished, as they should be . . . The economic growth of a dimension [unlike anything before it] and a society that took half a billion people out of poverty? *Of course they're proud of it!*'

— CHAPTER 19 —

ROSS GARNAUT

W HEN YOU'RE IN THE SOLAR AND BATTERY BIZ AND South Australia is faltering in its ability to deliver reliable energy and has a hundred mill to throw at renewables to fix it, well, you're a man with his beak to the grindstone trying to get a piece.

Hawke's former chief economist, Ross Garnaut, AO, who would lay the foundation for most of Labor's economic reforms in the eighties and nineties that would ensure prosperity for the following decades, is CEO of Zen Energy. And right now, Zen is locked in a righteous commercial battle with tech superman Elon Musk and his company Tesla for the contract to build a vast battery farm in South Australia.

Zen had been working with the South Australian government behind the scenes for months trying to drag the deal over the line, and then Musk had stolen headlines with one simple tweet: *Tesla will get the system installed and working 100 days from contract signature or it is free. That serious enough for you?*

When I arrive at the Zen HQ, I tell the cab driver to wait

while I re-examine the company's address. Instead of planting me in front of an office building, I'm outside a pretty federation house backing onto parkland in the inner Melbourne suburb of Carlton. A slim woman with short grey hair and wearing a T-shirt and jeans tends to a healthy vegetable garden facing the road. In the autumn sunshine, it's a picture of serenity. *Zen*.

A call confirms the address. The woman in the garden is Garnaut's wife Jayne. She beckons for me to enter, climbing out of the garden and offering a hand blackened by dirt. Garnaut, she explains, has been doing the ABC's AM program and is on his way back from the studio.

Jayne leads me into a small lounge room – or perhaps library is a more fitting description. Almost a thousand books are arranged on floor-to-ceiling shelves, eight shelves high, three wide. If I were to read them all, would I be as well-informed as Mr Garnaut, whose report to the Hawke government – *Australia and the Northeast Asian Ascendancy* – resulted in the final smashing of trade protection? Who was Australia's ambassador to China? Whom Hawke praises as the co-architect of his government's economic reforms?

In a kitchen off the library and in three bedrooms-cum-offices of this little zero-emissions hive, men and women – most in the climate change warrior uniform of check shirt and jeans – peck away at laptops.

Garnaut arrives, apologises for being late, falls into a lounge chair and asks about my book.

Hawke. Legacy. Reminder. Etc.

He grins. 'So it's about Australia's best prime minister.'

A week before, Hawke had described Garnaut as his 'soul mate' and said the pair were working on a 'very important' paper on global warming to be released later in the year.

Garnaut, who is seventy years old, wears the mandatory check shirt (with an iPhone 6 and pen in the breast pocket) and dark jeans, and his crown is topped with a hairstyle that is best described as serious-economist-turned-save-the-world-energy-salesman chic.

I tell Garnaut that on the way over from the city the cab driver had asked who I was interviewing. When I said it was Ross Garnaut, Hawke's economic adviser in the heady days of floating the dollar, deregulating the banks and so forth, he turned to me and said, 'Nah, mate. Wasn't Hawke or your bloke. Keating did everything.' Which I repeat to Garnaut.

'Keating has put *huge* effort into rewriting history.' Garnaut smiles, something he does more to add emphasis to a statement than to indicate pleasure. 'He's got the huge advantage that he didn't have much formal education and that affects his sense of objective historical reality. So, with Paul there is a bit of a sense of: *what I think is real* is *real*. And history is the story that's told. He was a great storyteller and that had political value, but the economic reforms wouldn't have happened without Hawke. They may or may not have happened without Keating. I think his strengths were greatest as treasurer working *within* the broader political framework established by Bob. His achievements as prime minister, much less lasting or prominent.'

Can you support your claim that Hawke was Australia's best prime minister?

'Well,' says Garnaut, 'I'm *very* interested in the question of Australian leadership and I've read just about all the biographies about all of them. But he changed Australia's views of what was possible in public policy. They go well beyond economics to education, to foreign policy, to health, the reintroduction of Medicare after Fraser had got rid of it. Some people might've been a little bit shy of that after Whitlam introduced it and was criticised for it, but Bob brought it back and this time it *stuck*.'

What else?

'He changed the environment of industrial relations in

Australia, which had been a very, very contentious and com-bative one. Quite a few areas of social policy: the introduction of family allowances, much more tightly means-tested social security so that we were able to finance much further in effectively targeting low-income people.'

And the big economic reforms, of course.

'The achievements were very considerable and the part-nership between Hawke and Keating was very effective. It had a new approach to macro-economic policy: the very difficult reforms on tax that previously were thought to be too hard. It was a major revamping of the tax system. And he achieved all of that. Change is hard politically and all while being re-elected four–nil. As a win-loss ratio, it's equal with a few who won one and didn't lose any, but when you look at the magnitude as well as the ratio, it's unparalleled. Menzies, of course, lost one-and-a-half elections.'

I tell Garnaut that Howard had said the Hawke govern-ment's success could be attributed to a non-obstructionist opposition.

'Well, that's true in part,' says Garnaut. 'Probably the most difficult and the central economic reform was the removal of nearly all protection. And that, at first, wasn't bipartisan. By the end it was. Hawke started educating the community for major reductions in protection from his first month in office. But it was very strongly the view that if you wanted permanent changes that stick, you don't take people by surprise. Public education is the key to it, so you talk about it. Get people used to the idea, and so when change comes they understand it and you don't get a backlash.'

Garnaut says Hawke used Whitlam's sudden decision to cut tariffs by 25 per cent in 1973 as a model of what not to do. It made imports cheaper, good, but blew a hole in local manufac-turing. Not so good.

'Fraser and the opposition made hay against it and there was no protection against it because there was no understanding in the community about it,' says Garnaut. 'Hawke went about a big program of public education in his speeches and his press conferences. He talked to relevant groups, trade unionists, business and community groups right from the beginning. And the reforms of tariffs started at the beginning. At first industry by industry, then a big, across-the-board tariff cut in '88 and the biggest of all in '91. And these huge changes occurred with very little negative political reaction. Now, looking at Australian history before Hawke one would've thought that was not possible – and he did it.'

Hawke says you were a co-architect of the government's economic reforms, I tell him.

'Bob's role as prime minister was essential, my role wasn't. I was replaceable. But I thought all those things had to be done. To be honest, when I went to work for Bob I didn't expect that what we went about achieving would be possible. He thought it was possible.'

How grave were the economic challenges the Hawke government faced in 1983?

'It was a depressing time. The highest unemployment since the Great Depression – at that time; it went a bit higher in the '91 recession. But up till then it was the highest we'd had. And we still had high inflation. That's a pretty big achievement. High inflation and record high unemployment. That's what Fraser left. And, more importantly, there was despair and pessimism, not much of a feeling that we could get out of it. [Plus] great clashes within society between organised labour and business but also between established interests and the broader community. Books were being written about that confrontational culture being part of what Australia was. So not only were the immediate political problems difficult but there was a general pessimism that we could find our way out of them. And one of the great achievements of the Hawke leadership was he turned all that around.'

On the flipside, Garnaut, who was chairman of BankWest (after a stint as Australia's ambassador to China) by the time of the 1991 recession, regards it as the grand failure of the Hawke government as it oversteered to correct the late-eighties boom. Employment scratched 11 per cent. Families lost their homes as interest rates soared. Major financial institutions, including the State Bank of Victoria, the State Bank of South Australia, the Teachers Credit Union of Western Australia, the Pyramid Building Society and merchant banks Tricontinental and Rothwells, failed. Australia wasn't alone, of course. Of the eighteen OECD countries of relative economic heft, seventeen of them went into recession in the nineties, ten worse than Australia's. But still. Despite Keating describing it as the 'recession we had to have', Garnaut says it wasn't inevitable.

'Late one night, chewing the fat, long after he ceased to be prime minister, I said to [Hawke] that was his biggest failure as prime minister,' says Garnaut. 'And we talked about how that had happened and he said that he hadn't been aware how vulnerable the economy was as we tightened monetary policy through the year and a half leading up to the recession. That was a period after the breakdown of relations between Bob and Paul, affecting how their offices communicated.'

Are you suggesting that it was the breakdown of relations between Hawke and Keating that caused the recession?

'Well, it meant that Bob didn't have access to alternative advice in relation to Paul and the treasury advice. And I think the breakdown in relations might've contributed to that.'

Could the recession have been avoided?

'First of all, there was excessive monetary expansion after

the financial crash of '87, so the origin of the recession was in that excessive expansion. And then there was an overreaction to the inflationary effects of that expansion.'

Briefly, I forget my high school economics and the fundamental difference between monetary and fiscal policy. Monetary works the interest rates lever. Fiscal turns on the government spending spigot. So when I suggest that it was massive cuts in government spending that dragged Australia down the hole, Garnaut smiles indulgently and gently corrects my mistake – it wasn't *government spending* – and repeats, 'Could it have been avoided? You'd have had to have started avoiding it in the boom. That's when it got out of hand. But then we undoubtedly overdid the tightening. It was a mistake that, in retrospect, various people played a role in. They sought to justify it on the grounds that it ended inflation so it was worth it. They didn't know that they were getting the highest unemployment in Australia since the Great Depression.'

I remember it well. Squeezing into ill-fitting, $15 shirts and polyester pants and pounding the streets with my hand-written (and mostly confected) CV trying to get a job. Any sort of job. It didn't have to be meaningful or even vaguely satisfying.

A painter with Main Roads? A teller in a suburban bank? I'd have taken either if there weren't 200 other kids panting at the door for the gig.

'Shocking. Damaging period,' says Garnaut. 'A pity. And while one can say it's the treasurer's job, everything is the prime minister's job. So if the treasurer is causing a recession, it's the prime minister's job to stop him.'

As Hawke's chief economist between 1983 and 1985, were you caught in the middle of the great tension between Hawke and Keating?

'The great tension came later. At the beginning, we were a very happy family, with Paul recognising that Bob understood the economic issues more confidently and was coming to talk to him about everything,' says Garnaut. 'But it was clear right from the beginning that Paul was very ambitious; nothing unusual about that. People who get to that position need to be, otherwise they wouldn't have got there. He wanted to be prime minister. My view is he recognised that he would have difficulty in becoming prime minister from opposition, from winning an election, and so his best chance of being prime minister was to succeed Bob in office. And as the years went by, he became desperate about that. But I think that the feeling that he had to succeed Bob in office was there from the beginning.'

Keating says Hawke sleepwalked through his final seven years as prime minister. Is that your experience?

'No, that's fantasy. The really interesting thing is Paul's done such a successful job in promulgating that view. I think that might be partly the way Paul came to office. He had to justify taking down the most successful prime minister in Australia's history – won four elections, never lost one. And similar things happened to a couple of earlier prime ministers who were dragged down by people on their own side. I think [Australia's first prime minister] Edmund Barton was a much more substantive figure than he was later recognised as being, and he was really pushed out by Deakin. People associated with Deakin were quite effective in diminishing Barton. That phenomenon when someone tears down someone from their own party, they sort of have to psychologically diminish the person they tore down to justify what they did.'

Garnaut first encountered Hawke when he was working as a research assistant during university vacations at the New

Guinea Research Unit in Port Moresby. The young economist would often stop by the Arbitration Court hearings where Bob was arguing the case for indigenous workers to be paid the same as their white counterparts.

'He was already a major national figure,' says Garnaut. 'Like lots of Australians, I was very interested in this well-educated, articulate person who seemed to be able to connect very well with the Australian people. He connected very well with the Papua New Guineans he worked amongst as well. For me, he was an impressive Australian.'

Had Hawke arrived at the same economic conclusions as you by the time you were hired in '83, or did you swing the PM to your way of thinking?

'He called me on his first Monday in the job and told me he wanted me to come to work as his economic adviser. His first question: "Is there anything in our platform that gives you any doubts whether you'd be comfortable in the job?" And he said, "Before you answer that, let me say, you need not be worried about the rather protectionist stuff in the party platform – we won't be doing that, nor will we be suddenly cutting tariffs. We'll be starting from the beginning to prepare the community for change that has to happen. You needn't worry about that. We're in the same boat on that one. Is there anything else?" And I said, "Well, I'm a bit worried about your whole macro-economic platform. You promised to hugely expand public expenditure to stimulate the economy, but over the last year Malcolm Fraser has given the economy the biggest stimulus in history, and if we give it any more then the top will blow off the place!" And Bob said, "You needn't worry about that either. I've absorbed the treasury briefings and we realise that the job is to pull back the anticipated budget deficit rather than expand it." So he established that there was no barrier to my joining him. But, in terms of the question you asked me, trade liberalisation was there from the very first conversation.'

Why does Hawke regard you as a soul mate?

'Bob's political philosophy is one that I grew up with and shared. It was a view of Australia as essentially an egalitarian society in which we could be creative. We had lots of talents and capacities for individual initiatives, but it wouldn't all work unless the fruits of economic success were being shared equitably. Bob held those views . . . strongly, more clearly, unequivocally and strongly, than other political leaders of my adult life.'

Do you and Hawke often talk about the fate of the species?

'We do a bit. We often talk about foreign policy, about the international scene. Bob's going on eighty-eight and is still very clear-headed, very well-informed, very interesting to talk to about foreign policy, China, US development, US–China relations, Europe, the rest of Asia, how it all fits together, what threats there are to peace, what threats there are to democracy.'

What threats to our western societies do you and Hawke see?

'Now, Bob's pretty optimistic that with good leadership, for all of the weakness of our contemporary political culture, it could still be pulled together. I don't *disbelieve* that, but I think some of the problems of our political culture have become pretty big. For example, the question of money politics, the influence of money over policy in the democracies, but especially in the United States and Australia.'

On the theme of optimism, I tell Garnaut that Hawke is optimistic – publicly, at least – about Trump. Garnaut smiles . . . although it might be more of a wince.

'I don't think he's gone overboard with enthusiasm. He knows the risks of Trump and the limitations of Trump. But generally Bob's optimistic about what is possible through effective leadership in our democracy. And I must say that at times historically when he's been more optimistic than me, he's been right. [That was] certainly the case with the period in his cabinet. On a number of issues he tackled them head-on and appealed to the better angels of the electorate's nature – and *won*.'

Such as in 1988, when the Coalition opposition revealed their One Australia policy calling for an end to multiculturalism and a slowing-down of immigration from Asian countries.

'I do believe that if in the eyes of some in the community it – Asian immigration – is too great,' said Howard, 'it would be in our immediate-term interest and supportive of social cohesion if it were slowed down a little, so that the capacity of the community to absorb was greater.'

In parliament a few weeks after the policy launch, Hawke unequivocally condemned the opposition leader.

'One of the great and rare distinctions of Australian political leadership in the last generation has been its bipartisan rejection of race as a factor in immigration policy,' said Hawke. 'This has been a triumph of compassion over prejudice, of reason over fear, and of statesmanship over politics. Twenty-two years ago my party, the Australian Labor Party, disowned its own historic White Australia policy, and the government led by Harold Holt, to its everlasting credit and honour, abolished the White Australia policy and began to dismantle the administrative machinery of discrimination.'

Hawke wanted to make it *very clear* that he wasn't accusing Howard of racism or of being a racist. His motives were much worse, said Hawke. Howard was a cynical opportunist, pulling out the threads of cohesion from the fabric of society, and all for a swag of dirty votes.

'His polling shows that there is this prejudice in the community and he has unleashed within his coalition and within the wider community the most malevolent, the most hurtful, the most damaging and the most uncohesive forces. Far from "one Australia" he has guaranteed a divided Australia.'

According to Garnaut, 'It wasn't certain that Hawke's position would be supported electorally. Bob was clear that it was right and that's why he was doing it. But it was clear to Bob that he would win. And he did!'

What do you think was Hawke's finest achievement in office?

'Historically, the most important for the country was paving the way for a successful multicultural, multiracial Australia by maintaining non-discriminatory immigration through a large-scale immigration program. Now, White Australia being the defining idea of Australia from Federation until the sixties, it took the initiatives of four prime ministers to change that. First of all, Holt, who made it less rigid. A university teacher from Hong Kong could now, if he got a job at the university of Melbourne, come in, whereas it was impossible before. A Japanese or Chinese or Indian who married an Australian could come in after Holt. But it was just a trickle. Whitlam abolished discrimination in immigration but greatly reduced the size of the immigration program so almost no one came in. The first large-scale Asian migration was through Fraser. Indochinese refugees. Vietnam. Cambodia. Laos. Historically, that was enormously important.'

So Hawke was just continuing Fraser's policy?

'No, he expanded it. Fraser's great contribution was to preside over a large refugee program. Hawke, being prime minister for eight years, and followed by Keating to continue those policies, he had long enough to bed down those programs. The bedding down of non-discriminatory immigration, I think, was essential for Australia's future. Central for our place in the Asian region. And the opening-up of the economy. But to do both of those things and to have Australians *comfortable* about them within a social democratic framework, so that it was consistent with Australian egalitarian values – that, broadly stated, is the Great Achievement.'

Do you believe Hawke was able to sell the policies because Australians viewed Hawke as one of them? He was, after all, a vastly different man to Fraser or Whitlam.

'Overwhelmingly, Australians were confident Bob was an Australian who shared their values and would work in their interests. So if he did something, he wasn't selling them out.'

Do you think Fraser would've had a different result?

'I don't think he could've done it. I don't think Turnbull could've done it. I don't think Abbott could've done it. I don't think Howard could've done it.' Garnaut's voice goes husky; passion brings out the burrs. 'And Paul couldn't have done it because Paul was a different personality. People didn't think he shared in their values, and his win-loss ratio was one–one. And the one was against John Hewson. And John, who is a good mate of mine, recognised himself as the most unelectable leader of a major party!'

Tell me about the report you prepared for Hawke in 1989, *Australia and the Northeast Asian Ascendancy*. When it came out it was viewed as so radical you were threatened with an unpleasant death by neo-Nazis, and branches of BankWest, of which you were the chairman, were daubed in white supremacist graffiti.

'It was the first policy-related document in Australia ever to talk about Australia having complete free trade. I talked about large-scale migration from China being a normal part of our story. No one had talked about it quite like that before and I got some negative reactions.'

It's not an exaggeration to say the report defined the final couple of years of the Hawke government. Are we still benefitting from those reforms?

'Bob ceased to be prime minister at the end of 1991, just after the recovery got underway. We haven't had a recession since then. We're the only country in the developed world that hasn't had a recession since then. And I think the reforms were pretty important to that. The decade after his prime minister-ship we went through the longest period of productivity growth in Australian history. We were top of the OECD of developed countries in productive growth and economic performance for the next decade, and we'd been down the bottom for the ninety years before that. [But] we've gradually lost the benefits of that period. We're not doing as well now.'

Why not?

'I call it the Great Australian Complacency of the Early Twenty-First Century.'

How do Hawke's four terms in office over eight years compare to Howard's five terms over eleven?

'Well, the period of the Hawke government was notable for structural reform, setting up Australia for the future. Now the early years of the Howard government, he continued some of that but gradually lost momentum, and since 2001 we haven't had any lasting productivity raising reform. The Reform Era came to an end, really.' Garnaut sounds wistful. 'And we entered the Great Australian Complacency of the Early Twenty-First Century, where vested interests gradually established dominance over policy. Governments were less and less inclined to make decisions in the public interest. They responded more and more to short-term political pressures. Through the twenty-first century, we've seen a gradual wearing away of that period of great dynamism and government in the public interest. We still retain *a lot* of the benefits of that period, we're still a much more dynamic and flexible society than we were and would've been, but it's no longer a politi-cal system capable of addressing hard questions – and, when changes need to be made, *doing* them, and making them stick. That's the big difference now. And if we compare Hawke with the Howard period, we lost that capacity during the Howard period. I roughly date the turning point as the beginning of the twenty-first century.'

Do you share Hawke's enthusiasm for making Australia a repository for the world's nuclear waste?

'I don't share it as a passion,' he says. 'But Bob's right. For densely populated countries like China or India, where it's not so easy to have a lot of renewable energy, [where they] don't have the huge open spaces we have here, the role of nuclear is potentially very important in climate change mitigation. If you think that nuclear has a role for all those reasons, then helping them do that is *valuable*. Australia does have the geology to support that.'

Garnaut might be down for hitting climate change in the guts, but he's been in the game long enough to know it's a hell of a sell, even for a master salesman like Hawke.

'It'll be a lonely crusade,' says Garnaut. '[South Australian premier] Jay Weatherill tried to put that forward and found it a heavy road to hoe.'

This isn't an exaggeration. Weatherill created a 'citizens' jury' of 350 South Australians to consider opening their state to the storage of nuclear waste. An overwhelming two-thirds majority rejected the idea of receiving 138,000 tonnes of used fuel over seventy years, despite the vast employment opportunities and a $51 billion windfall for the state. Memories of Chernobyl might have started to fade, but then Fukushima had come along to keep alive the nightmarish scenario of a nuclear disaster.

Longshots aside, and even if Hawke fails to get it across the line during his lifetime, Garnaut repeats what he told me at the beginning. Hawke *was* Australia's greatest prime minister.

'He showed us we could make *our* democracy in a way that worked for all Australians.'

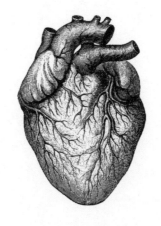

— CHAPTER 20 —

BLANCHE

IN THE EARLY SUMMER OF 1978, ACTU PRESIDENT BOB Hawke, who had just turned forty-nine years old and was married to Hazel Masterson, requested the hand in marriage of the award-winning writer Ms Blanche d'Alpuget, thirty-four and married to Tony Pratt.

Inside an unlovely Canberra motel, the sort characteristic of the clandestine affair, Hawke leaned his head on the unplastered wall and said that he was unhappy at home, and had had a dream the night before that convinced him he should leave his wife.

The dream involved another lover – a gorgeous, rich Swiss blonde nicknamed Paradiso. And although Blanche was prone to jealousy when it came to Hawke's affairs ('Jealousy is one of the most terrible corrosive emotions. It really is misery-causing,' says Blanche), the pair could talk openly about Paradiso because she lived in Europe.

'Theirs was a very romantic relationship because she was married to this really rich and much older guy and Bob had the hots for her but didn't think he'd get anywhere. And he invited her back to his hotel and suddenly she just put her arms around him,' says Blanche, who lunched with Paradiso two years later while in Europe researching *Robert J. Hawke*, the book that would help propel Hawke into the ALP leadership.

'We got on very well. She had a huge seventeenth-century house and invited me to stay next time I came to Switzerland. There was a strong sisterly feeling between us. I loved that she read [German poet] Schiller to Bob.'

In Hawke's dream, the roulette wheel had spun and the ball landed on Blanche. It meant he had to marry her – whatever the cost.

'He realised that for both of us it was a huge step,' says Blanche. 'Louis was six and his kids were teenagers and already very troubled. Their parents' bad marriage had made life very difficult for those children. But more than anything, being the children of a rock star ...'

Was tough?

'Terrible – *terrible*! You just can't get away from being in the shadow of the giant.'

What were your feeling towards Hazel, then Hawke's wife of twenty years? Did she enter your thoughts at all?

'I didn't have any because he never talked about it, which I really appreciate. Neither of us ever talked about our spouses to each other. We would have both considered that dishonourable. I had no idea what she was like. She had no public profile.'

Blanche, whose own eleven-year marriage was 'cactus' ('Usual story, hanging in there for the kids'), told Hawke she'd think about the offer over the two-month Christmas break, when family commitments meant pressing pause on the affair.

How did Hawke react when he offered Blanche the keys to his kingdom and everything within it and she said *maybe*?

'Well,' Blanche says – three decades older and still the most beautiful gal in most rooms – 'Bob was so drunk that if it was put before a jury he would've got off. In the sober light of day he was probably relieved.'

Blanche wallops the air with laughter then pauses to reapply her lipstick (the appropriately named 'Pink Dragon' by Estée Lauder).

While Blanche gussies up, slide onto the leather banquette of this Japanese restaurant so we can inspect the old broad a little closer. How does she look in the autumn of 2017?

Ageing is tedious and difficult, of course, but Blanche has trod an elegant middle road between carpet bombing her face and whatever else with surgery and toxins and allowing the years to pass relatively gracefully. Her own mother, she says, looked twenty years younger her whole life until she hit eighty when, suddenly, she looked eighty. Blanche presumes the same thing will happen to her. For the moment, though, in a tight-fitting blouse with detachable cravat and pale blue pants (part of a suit), with Bally heels, pearl earrings, wide blue eyes, pink lips and glossy yellow hair, she is a flamboyant locomotive billowing a teenage energy.

When the final touches of paint have been applied, I ask a damn stupid question.

'How many men have told you they loved you?'

Blanche is startled. You might as well try and count the stars in the sky.

She thinks about it, shakes her head, and answers with a starting point rather than a number.

'Since I was twelve,' she says, and tells me about her neighbour – a fifty-four-year-old district court judge notorious for the harsh sentences he gave sex offenders – who turned a stolen kiss into a two-year love affair.

After an initial encounter at her front door one afternoon, the judge would walk Blanche home from school and kiss her madly behind the cover of trees. She'd follow him into his kitchen while his wife entertained guests with their new television set and fall into his arms. The pair would drive in his glamorous Rover to secluded parts of Sydney, where he'd negotiate her school uniform and stroke her.

'I was in no danger of losing my virginity,' says Blanche. 'I was too young at the time to know what an erection was, but years later realised he was impotent. I've wondered since if "inappropriate touching" by older men is perhaps due to impotence, to their yearning to regain potency by contact with vital, young flesh.'

Initially Blanche adored the thrill of these secret meetings, but the affair fizzled out when Blanche began to see her lover as a desperate old man. It reached its nadir when Blanche visited the judge in his chambers, long after the affair had ended. He fell to his knees and thrust his hands between her legs. Instead of feeling desire, she suddenly saw a 'silly old goat in a white horsehair wig'.

Despite the fact she was well below the age of consent during the affair, Blanche doesn't consider herself a victim. But when she wrote about it in an essay called 'Lust', which appeared in Ross Fitzgerald's 1993 compendium *The Eleven Deadly Sins*, she was 'publicly caned for it. One man wrote a polite note saying he thought it an impossible piece of imagination: no member of the judiciary would do such a thing. Ha!'

In 1961, aged seventeen, Blanche ran away to Melbourne with LS, an illegal Polish immigrant, 'a wild man from Warsaw, a defector, escapee from Stalinism, writer, drinker of vodka, dancer of Cossack dances (when drunk), speaker of outlandishly-fractured English, an enchanted being.' That affair ended when her parents called in the police and had her lover handcuffed and dragged away. Blanche's father, the swashbuckling yachting journalist Louis d'Alpuget, told her the cops had shown LS a pistol that had been used in a recent armed robbery.

'Go near the girl again and your fingerprints are on it,' they said. LS fled to San Francisco. Blanche never saw him again.

Nine years later, Bob Hawke walked into her life.

The lovers met in 1970 at a party for expats in Jakarta, where Blanche was living with her first husband, Tony Pratt. The pair sat together in a swinging chair and spoke intently about trade unionism, geopolitics and the state of Indonesia while the party swirled around them.

Blanche's immediate impression was of a man who was 'physically nothing special' but 'so clearly a man of very forceful courage and character. He made a great impression on me psychologically. He was interested in everything. I knew a lot and he was really interested in what I had to say.' Afterwards, Blanche wrote a letter to her mother about a 'fabulously exciting' man she'd just met called 'Robin' Hawke, someone with this 'great big energy field'.

Blanche points out that at this point she was 'really' in love with her husband and that she wasn't looking at other men.

Still, this was the swinging seventies, when the pill promised absolute freedom long before the death sentence guaranteed by AIDS. Blanche writes, 'I had had many lovers, had been in love often and had once cried over a man. I loved my husband, whom I'd met when I was seventeen, and felt fiercely loyal to him. In the decade that we journeyed together we had both taken side trips, but we were mindful of each other's feelings, and discreet.' But nothing happened with Hawke.

The following year, again in Jakarta, as another boozy party of expats raged with debate over the Vietnam War, Hawke found Blanche and announced (perhaps too loudly given his fourteen-year-old daughter Sue was in earshot), '*I'd like to make love to you.*'

'He *was* very drunk,' says Blanche.

Four years passed before Blanche saw Hawke again. She was researching *Mediator,* her biography of Sir Richard Kirby, the longest-serving president of the Australian Commonwealth Conciliation and Arbitration Commission. Hawke, as advocate for the ACTU, had appeared innumerable times before Kirby, so she requested an interview.

Was she nervous, was she excited, about seeing Hawke again?

'I was *very* nervous and *very* excited.'

The pair met in Melbourne, at Hawke's ACTU office. At the conclusion of the first interview he invited Blanche to lunch at the pub next door where 'with mutual, wordless consent it was agreed we would become lovers as soon as possible – which happened to be in a different city the following night.'

It wasn't an all-nighter and Blanche, whose son Louis was four years old, regarded the liaison as one of her occasional side trips. Soon, though, the one-off turned into a semi-regular affair. They met every three weeks to a month, whenever they happened to be in the same city. In the interim, there were no phone calls, no contact.

'I knew he had a lot of interests,' says Blanche.

How did you know?

'Partly intuition, partly gossip. It built up bit by bit until, finally, the penny dropped. It's not something that you particularly want to face about your lover. The evidence accumulated, so I had to accept it. I wasn't going to let it carry me away until he got very serious, which was in '78, so that was eighteen months into the relationship.'

Were you consumed by thoughts of Hawke in bed with other gals?

'I didn't ever imagine what he would be doing with them. I always had the intuition that of all the women I was his favourite. I had nothing to base that on other than intuition. And maybe wishful thinking.'

When did you tell your husband about Hawke?

'By 1978 I'd told him, and he was terribly angered, very, very angered and jealous.'

Well, I say, it is a damn hard thing for a man to take. His wife shacking up with the most popular man in Australia. A master swordsman whom even the prime minister's wife, Tamie Fraser, admitted to finding sexy.

'Even the Queen did!' purrs Blanche.

How do you know?

'The way she treated him. She likes men . . .'

When did you confess to each other that it was love?

'He started telling me fairly early on . . .'

How early?

'Probably '76.'

Was it pillow talk? Dinner talk?

'Both. In his case pillow talk. In my case dinner talk. In a Canberra restaurant one night, I told him I'd die for him.'

I ask her to describe Hawke on the booze. Was it a gradual progression from life of the party and dazzling conversational-ist to mean drunk?

'You've got to remember,' says Blanche, 'our relationship was clandestine. I'd just see him when he had too much to drink. I'd see him drink too much and then become paranoid. That was the really difficult thing.'

Was he paranoid of being caught?

'No! Paranoid about *everybody*! *Everything!* Which comes out of guilt. He was even paranoid once, I remember, about *me*. That I might be some sort of *spy* or something.'

One of Malcolm Fraser's famous harem of spies?

'Yeah, for the government. Had he not been a bad drunk, had he not been a nasty drunk, he could've gone on drinking. Except he wouldn't have done his job very well. But he always main-tains he wasn't an alcoholic. I think he *was* an alcoholic. But he had that enormous and strong determination to go dry.'

When you say bad drunk, do you refer to the sort who calls the ALP leader Bill Hayden a 'lying cunt with a limited future'?

'Well, that's a good example. Some people get cute and cuddly and funny when they're drunk. He used to get sour and bitter. And, really, he was self-hating when he got drunk.'

Because of the weight of his affairs?

'Because his mother, who was the most important person in his development, made him promise at the age of eight that he would never drink alcohol. And he'd been brought up with this thing, the demon drink. You must never drink! And so he had a very *guilty* conscience.'

You've described Bob as being not the kind of man to leave by himself in a different city for long. The very nature of his work meant that he'd often be in different cities. How did that affect your relationship?

'It didn't. I was writing,' says Blanche. 'The thing that made me very nervous when he wanted to marry me was that I hadn't had my first novel published. I thought, *He's just going to eat me up and this life that he leads is going to eat me up and I'll never get my career going.* When you're writing fiction, or non-fiction for that matter, you are so obsessed, so terrifically obsessed with it, that virtually everything else is secondary. There has to be an *absolute family crisis* to take your mind off that. His being in different cities was a relief. I didn't want to see him more often than I was.'

But your world changed when Hawke proposed.

'Yes, because it brought to the fore something that I'd been avoiding for a hell of a long time and that was the problems in my own marriage . . . And I took advice from this very old friend of mine, a shrink, and with him worked out that it wasn't that I wanted to go with Bob; I didn't. I wanted to leave Tony.'

A year later, Hawke stopped calling. Eventually he rang

and told you he wasn't going to divorce Hazel. How did you respond?

'He'd been so conflicted his doctor had sent him for a brain scan to see if he had a brain tumour. But I was just *shattered*. None of this is logical . . .' Blanche laughs. 'Because by then, even though I'd left my husband, I knew I didn't want to be with [Bob] anyway. I wanted to stay in Canberra with Louis. But to know that he was jilting me . . .'

A pause.

'I was suicidal.'

Briefly.

'Yes, it was brief. I decided to murder him instead. I thought that would be much more satisfying.'

Can you describe your fantasy of shooting your lover?

'Well I can't. Because I'd never used a gun. But I knew *exactly* how to use a knife.'

Can you describe your fantasy of killing Hawke with a blade?

'*Oh yes*! That would be an embrace and then . . . I don't know if you know, but with a knife you must always strike up to get through the ribs and to the heart.'

With gusto and a sudden ferocity, Blanche pantomimes jamming the Sabatier steel into Hawke.

That would've been a newsworthy event, I offer. Beautiful girl murders famous cheating stud.

'*Yessssssss*. And I had this thing, *Oh I'll just be able to write while I'm in jail*.'

Two years after the break-up and you're back tapping on his office door for what would become your most significant work. Did you really decide to write *Robert J. Hawke* because you felt the media representation of Hawke was cartoonish? Or was it because you longed to reconnect?

'Yes, and *no, no, no*. I didn't long to reconnect. I was very, very interested in the trade unions, having done the Kirby book, and what they'd contributed to Australian society. And I first wanted to do the biography of Albert Monk, Bob's predecessor [as ACTU president]. His wife wouldn't let me because she was wife number two and she didn't want people to know. And so it's never been written. It's a great pity because he kept copious notes, all in a very strange shorthand. But the trade unions formed a lot of the ethos, the values, of twentieth-century Australia.'

How did Hazel react when Bob told her you were writing his biography? How much did she know about the two of you?

'Well, I don't know. But he persuaded her that she should talk to me, and she did.'

How were those conversations?

'Somewhat strained. And she was, very reasonably of course, extremely hostile towards me. But she saw it as something that she ought to do. She suspected I was only doing it for money. She actually said that to me. Which wasn't the case. I was doing it out of the conviction that he was a very important force in the country and was not properly understood and presented.'

When the book, which detailed Hawke's infidelities, was released and she was asked how she coped with his myriad betrayals, Hazel told the *Sunday Press*, 'Of course there was hurt. That's not unusual. But it's gone. I suppose I coped in a very average way. I always felt it was just a phase . . . I didn't see it as the *core* of Bob.'

Most importantly, for all his popularity, the biography convinced the Labor Party he had the depth of experience necessary to become leader.

'It convinced two critical people, and they were on the national executive of the ALP. One of them was Lionel Bowen. The other was John Button. Both of them are dead. I'm sorry to talk about people who are dead, because they can't verify what

I'm saying to you, but it was really significant as far as swinging the vote. And you can't underestimate the *degree* of hostility in the caucus to him. He was an outsider. He didn't play by their rules. They'd done twenty years, man and boy before the mast, and here was this show pony who was going to waltz in and snatch everything. It was a hell-pit of jealousy and hatred. And it was only because they feared they were going to lose the election that they decided to change.'

You say that in January 1980, when you had your first interview for the book, you didn't talk about the past – but did you feel *something*?

Blanche pauses, suddenly coy.

'If you've had a really strong, physical, sexual connection with somebody, the energy from that is always present. And with it comes a degree of trust. So he could speak openly.'

Did something grow during those two-and-a-bit years working on the book? Did you sleep together? Oh god, I've gone Charles Wooley on you! Forgive me! But do tell ...

A long sigh turns to laughter. 'I'll let that one go through to the keeper! But I do need some more tea.' She signals to the waitress. '*Excuse me!*'

How did you feel when your book propelled Hawke to the leadership of the ALP and, ultimately, the prime ministership? You were in Israel, so you had time to think ...

'After doing a biography ... I'd had this experience once before, so when it happened again I knew it was normal, but by the end of doing the biography I was *so sick of him*. Honestly, you give so much of yourself to concentrating on this one person and when it's over you think, *thank god!* So, obviously, I was thrilled he'd won the election. I thought it was a *lay-down miserè* that he would. But I had moved on emotionally.'

Was that some sort of elevating feeling, that your book had helped put Hawke there?

'No. No. Not at all. By then I was completely engaged with Israel.' (Blanche was writing the novel *Winter in Jerusalem,* about a female screenwriter who returns to Jerusalem to reconnect with her father.) 'But then, thrillingly, he rang me up.'

What did he say?

'*G'day.*' Blanche hoots.

Did you immediately know who it was?

'Yes. Of course, there's a seven-hour time difference, so you're psychologically dislocated. He just asked after me and how it was in Jerusalem. I was very thrilled that he did ring up.' Blanche smiles at the memory. 'And he had to go to considerable lengths. God knows how he got my phone number.'

And you came back to Australia, you were living in Woollahra in Sydney, you found spirituality, you had boyfriends, a gorgeous life. Then, in November 1988, he called you again.

Blanche mimics Hawke calling. '*G'day.* I think that's how it always is with a very deep connection. You don't see someone for years and when you do nothing's changed.'

Hawke told me he'd never stopped thinking about you in that period.

'Really?'

And that the need to call you had become overwhelming . . .

'*Right.* He's never told me that.'

Eventually . . .

'There's a difference between – and it's taken me a long time to understand it – there's a difference between love and adoration. And adoration is on a higher level and a deeper level. And it takes longer to get there. But that, actually, is what we felt for each other. Adoration.'

How did your love affair part two differ from part one?

'I was still very cautious,' says Blanche. 'I'd been let down once. I wasn't going to take it seriously. I wasn't going to get into that same position of wanting to kill myself, kill him, howling for three days. And, I *did* have a couple of nice friends...' Her eyelids lower provocatively, her voice is like honey. 'Mmmm. Well, I was a free woman, I was divorced. But [with Hawke] it just intensified. It intensified. And a clandestine relationship when the secret service is involved is particularly exciting.'

These days, Hawke thanks Keating for taking the leadership as it opened the door for you and him to go public and, eventually, get married. How long after the second – successful – challenge did he call you and what did he say?

'It wasn't the successful challenge. He called me soon after the Kirribilli agreement [in November 1988, when Hawke promised he'd resign in favour of Keating shortly after the 1990 election].'

Did he tell you that, by virtue of his agreement with Keating, he was soon going to be free of all the obligations that had kept him married?

'No! He had no idea! He never confided to me about the Kirribilli agreement. I learned about it from the media like everyone else. No, he just wanted to take up the relationship again.'

But after the successful challenge...

'Well, that was three years later.'

Blanche was 'deep in the country' when Hawke lost his job to Keating. Still, through their intermediary, Hawke got through.

'He was in a very bad way psychologically,' Blanche says. 'For a long while. He was *really, really* cut up. Cut up by the party and cut up that he'd done so much for them and they'd turned around and stabbed him in the back. That's what he felt. But he'd made the agreement with Paul and he could've just realised he had to keep it. Of course, Paul had been stalking him from the day Bob had got the leadership. Initially those strains were very well papered over and they really did make a good team.'

And there were moments of love.

'Oh there were! Politicians are basically warlords at that level. I don't think I'm being romantic when I say there was a warrior love between them, how men who fight side by side feel about each other. They had that brother-I've-got-your-back connection. And that was very strong, that male love.'

Much is made of the schism between the two but not the love.

'And Paul had magnificent gifts which Bob didn't . . . parliamentary gifts. Paul was wonderful in parliament. Bob was never any good in the parliament. He was basically a barrister, and what you need as a lawyer is a different skill set . . . And Paul had been honing that since he was in swaddling clothes. And he pulled Bob's chestnuts out of the fire quite a few times.'

Did Hawke appreciate it?

'Yeah, although being a classic alpha male I'm sure it embarrassed him. Although now that he's older and cannot drive, he mentioned the huge advantage of having a car and driver. He said, "That's another thing for which we have Paul to thank." Because it was Paul, as PM, who pushed through the legislation that former PMs could have a car and driver. It was immensely useful for Gough, John Gorton and Fraser, and is now an essential for Bob.'

Was it Paul's line about not living at the arse-end of the earth and threatening to piss off to Paris that convinced Hawke to renege on the Kirribilli agreement?

'It wasn't just one thing. It was a *gazillion* small things. Snide remarks that Paul made to colleagues about Bob. He really started pulling as many bricks out of the wall as he could. Very active.'

In 1994, six years into their reignited affair, Blanche – an ambassador for CARE Australia – flew to Pakistan's North-West Frontier Province to write about the terrible deprivations of Afghanistan's female refugees. She'd arranged to meet Hawke in Hong Kong on the way home.

On the day of departure from Afghanistan, Blanche's flight from Peshawar to Karachi was cancelled, thereby creating a chain of missed connections. She arrived in Hong Kong a day late. Hawke was deeply suspicious of the delay.

'What's wrong?' she asked.

'Nothing,' he lied.

Hawke had checked the flights and was told there were no cancellations. He was convinced Blanche had found a lover.

'He was not angry or reproachful,' Blanche writes in *On Longing*.

> He was so heartsick he could barely summon the energy to speak. All the pain and agony of divorce, all the visions of happiness together, all our years of longing for each other shrivelled. In the end I said, 'You just have to believe me.' He couldn't. He was about to do something irrevocable to be with me, and the thought that I had deceived him was unbearable. Back in Sydney it was clear we'd come to the end of the road and, whimpering with grief, we said goodbye.

Tell me about 1994, when you missed the plane?

'Well, I was absolutely *appalled* that he didn't believe me. I was *truly appalled* and I thought, *Here we go again*. So I said that's it. Goodbye. He had rung the airline and the airline had said, "Oh no, sir, the plane took off!" and it was only through checking the story – I think he had to do it through the intelligence community – that he found out the truth, that the flight *had* been cancelled. And so then he was horrified [but] I was still adamant that I'd had enough and I wasn't going to cop it anymore.'

The pair's intermediary invited Blanche to dinner and pleaded Hawke's case. Told her Hawke was distraught, destroyed, that he couldn't concentrate, that he couldn't continue to live without her. Would she at least let him apologise?

Only over the phone, Blanche stipulated.

'And of course . . .' Blanche erupts into laughter. 'Foot in the door, isn't it!'

And he was charming?

'Oh yeah! And full of remorse that he'd not believed me.'

And the following year you were married.

'July '95.'

And not long afterwards, you left Hawke when he started drinking again.

'We were living in Northbridge and he got very drunk, got very angry,' says Blanche. 'He could be very snide and abusive, but was never ever – to me or anybody else – physical. And I'd said to him straight up: I can't cope with your drinking. Because he started drinking heavily again. As I said, he actually is an alcoholic. He will never say he is, because he successfully gave it up. These days he can keep his drinking down to an absolute minimum. But I think that comes with age. Anyway, I went to a friend's place and he didn't know which one.'

After the years of abstinence during his political career, was it '92 when Hawke got a taste for booze again?

'Yes, it was Hazel's birthday. They were living in the Ritz-Carlton [in Double Bay] and this vile Italian restaurateur had said, "It's Hazel's birthday! There must be champagne!" Bob was gone. I was appalled, because he came to see me a couple of days later and he smelled of grog and he was stupid and I thought, *I don't want this.*'

And after you left he squashed it down to one drink a day?

'Oh no. No, no, no. Look, it's terribly hard for alcoholics to drink in moderation. They have an on button but no off button. No, there were many more times when he would drink too much and I would shout at him and so forth. It was the only thing we ever argued about. And the kids, sometimes. *His kids.*'

You famously slapped his eldest daughter Sue in the Qantas

Club in 2011. Yet in the ABC's *Australian Story* episode on Hawke you appeared to be terrific pals. Was it all a confection for the cameras?

'It was partly a confection. The first thing to say is that I love Sue, and the feeling is mutual. But she's feisty, and we do argue. I thought she'd behaved *appallingly* towards me. She had stuff in women's magazines about how I'd written Hazel out of history and so forth, and I was really furious with her. I was sitting, minding my own business in the Qantas Chairman's lounge, when out of the blue she squatted down beside me and, all smiles, started to chat, as if we were the best of buddies. I thought, *I could wring your neck.*

'I warned her, "I'm not speaking to you. Go away." She was astonished but kept talking. I said a second time, "Go away." She wouldn't and seemed annoyed that I refused to speak to her.'

And then, slap, slap, slap, slap. Four times?

'Just two, front hand, backhand. She said, "How dare you do that?" and I replied, "Would you like me to do it again?" She turned to a group of six men who were sitting behind her to ask, "Did you all see that?" They buried their heads in their newspapers and became deaf. Bob was horrified when I told him. "You didn't! You didn't!" he said, holding his head. It was very bad form on my part. Of course I apologised to Sue later, and our affection for each other was, if anything, heightened.'

A salvo of satisfied laughter.

'I do have a temper,' says Blanche, 'and the contretemps was a storm in a teacup. But the barometric pressure for such storms comes from a deep seam of suffering in our culture that leads people to believe life is a zero-sum game. "You win. I lose." The Hawke divorce was pitch-perfect for this attitude, but really it was a win-win-win. Obviously, for Bob and me, but also for Hazel. She was liberated to be her own woman for the first time since her twenties. She escaped an ugly, dead marriage. She loved the view from the Northbridge house, but the rest of it was not so much to her taste. In moving to Castlecrag she got a house she loved and, as importantly, a garden she loved. She was always a mad keen gardener, but the Northbridge garden is a rainforest, a joy for fruit bats, possums and mountain goats. Not for human recreation. When I say it was win-win-win, I don't mean it was painless. For the three of us, there was plenty of pain. I thought of Hazel often . . . It sounds so corny, but it's true: I felt her pain. I should add, she herself said repeatedly she did not want to be seen as a martyr. She rejected the label as offensive . . . And life has pain, along with joy. Hazel had the joy of being wife of the Great Man.'

Ironically, you contributed to his greatness with *Robert J. Hawke*.

'I can't say that.'

But I can . . . Gareth Evans says your book *Hawke: The Prime Minister* caused the final rift between Bob and Paul. Is that true?

'No. The rift was at the time of the challenge. When Bob rang Paul regarding my tinnitus, Paul could not have been more friendly, and that was years after *Hawke: The Prime Minister* was published. That book was just a record of what people who had worked closely with Bob said. As I mentioned earlier, it was a long essay intended to be an addition to the original biography. I was able to talk to people who wouldn't talk to journalists, wouldn't have talked to any other writer, but talked to me.'

But Paul wouldn't talk to you?

'Paul wouldn't talk to me, no. I wrote to him and asked him. He was still very shirty with Bob. He's got that Irish thing. But the other thing that I didn't know at the time, and Bob didn't know at the time, was that just before he had to do the budget, Paul got very bad tinnitus. And since I've had tinnitus I know how terrible it is and how it makes you very, very ratty. That's why I'm wearing this thing.' She points to the orthodontic brace she wears to correct the misalignment of her jaw. 'So, he had this constant mental irritation. The poor man. Bob used to worry about it, "Ah, I wish I could do something for Paul, it's really driving him nuts," and I'm now saying, "Oh god, I hope this works because we're the same age and if it works for me, maybe it'll work for him."'

Have you spoken to him about it?

'I didn't speak to him directly. I spoke at length to his secretary. She took lots of notes and called me back and said, "Paul said, thank you very much." I think he's tried everything and has given up. And it's basically ruined his life. You can't enjoy life in a normal way. He can't leave the house without little earbuds because outside noise is so abhorrent.'

In the same book that angered Paul, you write about him being beautiful. Now, if someone emphasised my beauty in a book I'd forgive a multitude of sins.

'He *was* beautiful. And he had the most beautiful eyes. And elegant. And a knife fighter.'

Tell me about killing Bob if he were ever to 'lose his marbles'. What's your arrangement?

'None,' says Blanche flatly. 'I said to him, "Listen, unless euthanasia is legalised I'm not going to jail as a murderess."'

Do you talk to him, coach him, in any spiritual training for the day of death?

'We talk about it from time to time, and I remember years ago he said to me, "I'm going to be no trouble. I'll be like my dad. I'll go easily." I hope that's true. And the great thing is, since you started interviewing him, the nerves in his feet are growing back. It's a slow process but he's walking so much better than he was before. He's standing up straighter, his whole body is . . . returning.'

Do you ever imagine life without him?

'I'd be stupid if I didn't. I'd be unrealistic if I didn't.'

Allow me a final question, perhaps the most important question of all. What's the secret to taming a great and prolific lover like Hawke?

'Love.'

Long pause.

'Truly, it's love.'

— CHAPTER 21 —

TAPPING A KEG

T HE TWO THIRTY-SOMETHING AD AGENCY MEN, AUSTRALIANS who'd flown to Sydney from New York, where they now worked, arrived at Hawke's house in April 2016 with a business proposal.

Being ad guys, when they recall the meeting they say things like, 'We were really buttoned-up,' which means they were prepared, and they'd already sent a 'snapshot' of the idea to Hawke and his various people.

The men, David Gibson and Nathan Lennon, had decided to leave the ad business and start their own brewing company, and they wanted to name it Hawke's Brewing Co.

They'd landed on the name fifteen months earlier. It was Australia Day back home and Nathan, who's from Bondi Beach and suffers terrible homesickness, was looking through the glass wall of his office and across the gloomy East River to Brooklyn. Weather forecasters were predicting New York's worst-ever blizzard. 'Snowmageddon 2015', they called it.

Nathan and Dave knew that back home all their buddies would be on the beach, playing cricket, draining their eskies of delicious cold beers, the sun drying the saltwater on their backs.

Nathan looked at Dave and said, 'Mate, if you could have a beer with anyone right now, who would it be?'

Nathan calls himself a 'fan-boy' of Hawke but kept his dream drinking buddy to himself. He expected Dave would name one of their mates.

Instead, Dave turns around says, 'Hawkey! *Mate*. Who else?'

The pair started talking about how much they adored the former prime minister, how he defined their early lives and how he 'transcended politics to connect with everyone'. As commercial ad men, they marvelled at the terrific 'reach' he still has.

The conversation stretched into the idea of launching the little brewing company they'd been thinking about under the banner 'Hawke's Brewing Co'. The pair had just worked on the repositioning of a Nabisco subsidiary, the cracker brand Honey Maid. The two creative directors had helped reshape the brand as the cracker for the diverse family – the interracial, gay, tattooed rock family. It didn't matter how you got your kicks, Honey Maid was ready to sell you a box of wholesome crackers. What if they could give Hawke's Brewing Co. a similar socially conscious and feel-good backstory, this time with Australia's most popular prime minister?

They prepared their 'snapshot'. Sent it away. Hawke read it. Liked it.

So Hawke knew what was coming. A brewery. His name on it. But he wanted to feel them out. See if they were the kind of men he could do business with or have his name associated with.

Hawke received Nathan, Dave and a third partner from Australia, Luke Langton, at the dining table that adjoins the kitchen. It was 11 am, which is early for Hawke, who's done enough to warrant the pleasures of sleeping in until whenever the hell he wants, at least until the sun climbs over Seaforth and is soaking his north-facing bed in sunlight. Ever since his chest was sliced open and a pacemaker plugged in a few years ago, Hawke will sleep for at least ten hours, sometimes fifteen, a night.

As he takes his breakfast of black cherries, blueberries, pine nuts and milk, Hawke examines four newspapers, the *Sydney Morning Herald*, *The Australian*, the *Australian Financial Review* and the *Daily Telegraph* (or *Terrorgraf*, as Blanche calls it). The *AFR* is his favourite, but there's no point in being blind to alternative perspectives.

When the men arrive Hawke sweeps the table clear. Asks them what the deal is.

The trio – making the 'biggest pitch of our lives' – went into their spiel: brand positioning, brand pillars and so on.

Hawke already had his answer. If they could shovel his fee into Landcare, the volunteer organisation that had brought farmers and conservationists together a quarter of a century earlier and which he'd helped create, why not?

His suitors presented their master with a gift-wrapped box to celebrate.

'Cigars?' asked Hawke.

'Cubans.'

'You *bloody beauty!*' he whooped.

Hawke then told them to check out the house, stuffing all three into the tiny travelator that rattles down the side of the house and removes the need to negotiate the winding path through tropical jungle and down to Louis' boatshed.

They visited the games room with the full-sized snooker table and framed photos on the walls. There is Neil Armstrong saluting the camera on the moon ('To Prime Minister Bob Hawke, A memorable moment in history to be shared by all'). Hawke, dressed in Quiksilver and holding a surfboard, caught in an embrace with the world champion surfer Tom Carroll at Bondi Beach. Hawke and Alan Bond post-America's

Cup victory under a relief model of the famous *Australia II* hull and winged keel. Hawke belted in the face by a bouncer in 1984. An athletic Hawke playing tennis. Team photos of Hawke and various Prime Minister's XI cricket teams.

By the time they'd finished their tour, they found Hawke sunning himself on the terrace, one of the new cigars cracked.

He told them to grab a seat, and then he hit them with an hour-and-a-half of golf and cricket jokes and ribald stories. It was Hawke at his finest, raked in sunlight, a plume of cigar smoke, an adoring audience.

One year and two days later, the beer launches at a pub called The Clock in Sydney's Surry Hills. It is one of eleven hotels that will have Hawke's Brewing Co. on tap. (The Clock will sell out of its weekly, ten-keg allotment in twenty-four hours. Nathan and Dave deliver six more kegs, which run dry by the next day.)

It is also sixty-eight years since Hawke, aged nineteen, had his first beer. He was so riven by guilt at the time, but also so thrilled by the elevating effect of beer, he told his mother that he had started to drink and that he wasn't stopping. The conversation, he recalls, 'wasn't pleasant'. Ellie would pray every day that Bobby would eventually turn off the spigot.

And it wasn't as if he was born to drink. As one fellow student recalled, 'After two glasses of beer he would be whacked or throwing up in a way I've never seen before – it was an incredible cacophony, you'd think the whole world, including his feet, was coming up. But Bob was determined to improve as a drinker, as he was determined to improve at everything he did.'

But now, on 6 April 2017, at precisely 3.15 pm as per the press release, the veteran drinker Bob Hawke suddenly appears from around a corner. He is led to a tap and expertly draws the first Hawke's Brewing Co. schooner.

'How's that for a pour! A lovely beer,' he says.

Someone yells for Hawke to neck the beer in one go. He declines.

Hawke only drinks red wine these days, unless he's at the cricket or a golf club and the legend needs reinforcement. He wets his beak and points the schooner at the cameras, to a blizzard of flashes.

Hawke places the beer down on the drip tray and is handed a microphone. The old master, nearly ninety, plays to the crowd.

'One of the great challenges facing us is global warming,' he begins, voice an ominous dark bass. 'I'll do whatever I can through Landcare and other means to meet that challenge. But this is particularly exciting because it combines a couple of loves...'

The crowd loosens. A few pre-emptive laughs. They know what's coming.

'I've been known to enjoy the odd beer.'

The rooms laughs in unison.

'And a quick one!'

Now he's hitting form.

'The quickest ever!'

Howls! Whoops!

With the pack under his spell, he hands them the quandary of modern life.

'But I also love this country and I love the opportunity that is very much in our hands,' he says, mounting the pulpit. 'We live at an *absolutely* unique point in human history. For the first time in recorded history, because of the flowering of the technological and scientific genius of mankind, we are at a point where we can do one of two things. One: we can lift the standard and quality of life of every human being on this planet. Or, two: we can destroy life on this planet as we know it. Those are the two awesome paths before us. And in our small way, our enterprise is concerned with helping us make the right choice . . . '

The journalists, the photographers and the friends – including Hawke's stepson Louis, the Herculean trainer Ryan and his secretary, all of whom have seen the still-electric charisma before – are as captivated as a gang of twenty-something girls who've stumbled onto the event.

'Now,' says Hawke. 'We're going to be doing our best to ensure Australia and the world goes down that first path. And you can have a feeling of wellbeing as you sip your Hawke's Lager, knowing that as you sip that Hawke's Lager you'll be making a contribution to the environment and to your country. Help your country and have a beer at the same time!'

Another eruption of flashes. Cheers. Finger whistles. Drinking as a virtue!

The following morning, Sydney tabloid, the *Daily Telegraph* will front-page the event with the headline: FROM SILVER BODGIE TO SILVER TINNY.

The Times in London leads with: HAWKE PULLS A PINT AND IT'S GOT HIS NAME ALL OVER IT.

Landcare will estimate a reach of five million people through the PR surrounding the event, five times more than their next-most-successful launch with a corporate partner.

The old master walks off the stage. Job nailed.

— CHAPTER 22 —

HAWKE ROARS
AT DEATH . . .

F OUR DAYS AFTER THE BEER LAUNCH, I'LL GIFT HAWKE a final cigar, a $39 Davidoff that the proprietor helpfully cut for me with a gold blade and secured in a clear plastic bag.

'Went alright, didn't it,' says Hawke of an event splashed across every major newspaper in Australia, and enough abroad to confirm his universal appeal.

I haven't seen the old man look this pert or in this buoyant a mood since our interviews began ten months earlier. The virus that nearly took him out is long vanquished. The cold that had him in bed for a month has evaporated. Even the feet are threatening to kick back into life.

It's a good day. Windless. Late autumn. No clouds. The light bounces into Hawke's brown face from the white table and the white chairs.

It's a sublime setting for our final interview – which, I announce theatrically, is centred around his relationship with Paul Keating and, if we have time (unlikely given the dazzling material I've mined from a recent bio of Keating),

Hawke's musings on dying, death and the hereafter.

In November 2016, *Paul Keating: The Big-Picture Leader*, by political journalist Troy Bramston, was published. It's the first time Keating has cooperated with a journalist on a biography. The book is a 786-page forensic examination of a political animal whom Bill Hayden described as 'chilling' in his ambition. *The Australian*, for whom Bramston works, describes it as a 'hymn of praise to Keating'. I eat it up in a few days, so compelling, so cutting, are the references to Hawke.

A few months earlier, we'd talked briefly about Keating when I threw Hawke the question about the prime minister receiving guests, including his cabinet, in the nude.

'Absolutely untrue,' he said. 'It's bullshit.' He'd chortled and said, 'I think it's Paul trying to get one in.'

Then he grew reflective. 'I've told you many times, I genuinely feel sorry for Paul. You know, I genuinely do. It's not just a confected statement. In the history of federal politics he was outstanding. He did so many good things that it's a real pity he . . . Two things. One, that he's such a hater. He just hates! And he just wants to claim a bit more than he's entitled to.'

This time, Hawke's face drops when I mention the topic. I've been here enough to recognise a change in mood, however slight. A dark curtain rattles across the stage.

'Hmmmmmm. Right.'

I tell him I've read *Paul Keating: The Big-Picture Leader*. I found its references to you and your government compelling, I say.

Hawke is silent.

I have three pages of typed questions in front of me. The pages rustle awkwardly. The first question – about Keating leaning on journalist, and later premier of New South Wales, Bob Carr in 1978 to write damning stories about Hawke in the political weekly *The Bulletin* ('Is Hawke Finished?' and 'Hawke

Loses Ground Inside the Labor Party') – isn't going to fly while the door is closed. Instead, I start with breeze.

When was the last time you spoke to Paul?

'Aw . . . *aw* . . . a couple of months ago. He suffers very badly from tinnitus. It was really terrible for him. And Blanche has got it in recent time and we spoke to Paul and he was very, very helpful. I spoke to him then.'

Would you describe your current relationship as cordial?

'Yeah, he was very kind to me at the launch of the [2016 Labor election] campaign,' says Hawke. 'We obviously had our well-known differences, but I respect Paul greatly. He is without a doubt one of Australia's greatest treasurers and what I really did admire about him was that he had no formal education in economics and he applied himself and learned quickly.'

What were your primary differences?

'The difference between Paul and myself was he loved parliament. I didn't. I disliked parliament. I was used to appearing in the tribunal and the result of the hearing depended upon the quality of the argument. I won or lost the case on the basis of the argument. In the parliament, everything was decided in advance. Whoever was in government, they had the majority and they won. I could never get excited about parliament.'

It feels like Hawke is warming a little. I ask about the Carr stories and Keating's influence and ambition.

'Ah, well, the New South Wales blokes told me. They made the decision to support me and that upset Paul,' says Hawke. 'But the important thing when talking about the Hawke–Keating relationship is not to emphasise the differences we had but that we were a magnificent team and we did great things for this country.'

In 1982, Graham Richardson said, '[Keating] didn't like Hawke and he didn't like Hayden. He didn't think anyone should be leader except for him.' Keating also said, 'Bill is not a narcissist; Bob is a narcissist.' He felt with Hayden as leader there'd be a more orderly eventual transition to power after a 1983 ALP victory. What were your feelings towards Paul in the late seventies and early eighties? Did you regard him as a serious challenger? Was he prime ministerial material back then?

'Oh yes, I thought he had it. I had a leaning towards Kim [Beazley] because I thought he had a broader background. There's no doubt Paul was better equipped in the economics side. Kim was very good in foreign affairs and defence and competent in economics. But I think it's one of the greatest tragedies that after Paul had had his turn that Kim didn't get that 1998 election where he won the majority of votes. The subsequent history of Australia could've been quite different.'

Do you wish you had retired and pushed Beazley as your successor at the end of 1990? Hewson was beating you in the polls, you'd been in the job almost eight years, would it –

'Oh, no, no, no. I did what was the right thing to do.'

I remind Hawke that Beazley's popularity rating was vastly superior to Keating's in 1990: 51 to 28 per cent.

'Yeah, I know.'

To a Beazley contest, Keating had said, 'There would only be one hit in it!' He was that sure he would have knocked Kim out. How would that challenge have played out, do you think?

No response.

Oh, I'm dying. I remember what Paul Kelly had told me about interviewing Hawke.

'The key to interviewing Hawke is to trigger a spontaneous reaction on an important issue that has emotional resonance. Hawke is a very emotional person. And, particularly, you can see this on TV. If you can engage his emotions then it becomes utterly compelling. Utterly so.'

Cough. Rustle. I push a little more.

In 1991, the newspapers turned against you as leader en

masse. No major metro paper editorialised in favour of your remaining as prime minister. Voters, meanwhile, couldn't have been more pro-Hawke. *The Age* published a poll that found 66 per cent of voters said you'd be a better PM than Keating, who polled 18 per cent. Newspoll had Keating at 14, you at 61. Among Labor supporters, it was you 77 per cent to 17. How did the contradiction of opinion stack with you?

'Well, I had a long relationship with the Australian people,' says Hawke. 'It went right back to the time when I was representing Australian workers in the court then as head of the ACTU. And I *genuinely* like people, you know. I like mixing with them and I was more at ease with people than Paul was.'

How did Paul woo the press?

'The press enjoyed Paul. He was fun in parliament. They got more fun out of him than they did out of most politicians.'

In August '88, you appeared on the ABC's *The 7.30 Report* just after the budget and said, in a roundabout way, that Paul was good but, because of the depth of talent in your cabinet, he was replaceable. Was that a shot across the bow for Paul to pull his head in?

'Aw . . . no . . . it was just sorta . . . it was just a statement of fact that . . . but, look, I've always publicly and privately acknowledged how good Paul was . . .'

The afternoon following the appearance on *The 7:30 Report*, Keating saw Hawke in his office and told him, 'The relationship is over, dead and buried,' and, 'When I decide to come at you, mate, I'll take your head right off!'

According to Keating now, 'Had he not gone on the television set and said the day after the 1988 budget that he didn't need me anymore, then the leadership would not have formally arisen in 1988 and there would have been no Kirribilli agreement . . . So Bob brought it on by this streak of jealousy he has in his nature . . . the budget of 1988 went so well he couldn't contain himself. He had to say something mean.'

Hawke is irritated. To question his intention, his honesty and ethics never goes well. In an earlier, more vital epoch, he would've let me have it:

'It's a ridiculous question and you know it's ridiculous.'

'You're being a bloody pest.'

Or, 'I hope the standard of your questions improves.'

Today it's a mild lash, a light cane across the buttocks instead of the once-formidable cat-o'-nine-tails.

'All these sorta questions suggest that I didn't have respect for him,' say Hawke. 'I mean, he was a *very considerable treasurer and parliamentarian*! Very considerable.'

Were you worried after your comments that the government would lose its prized treasurer and parliamentary performer?

'Well, I was,' says Hawke, who, upon the urging of his Minister for Social Security, Graham Richardson, followed up *The 7.30 Report* interview the next night with a conciliatory piece on Ray Martin's *A Current Affair*, where he'd say, variously, 'I want him there, because it's very much in many respects a Hawke–Keating government' and that Keating's ambition to be leader was 'totally legitimate'.

And now: 'It was unpleasant, but it passed,' says Hawke.

In November the same year, you pledged to hand over the prime ministerial levers to Keating when you met with him, Bill Kelty and Peter Abeles, at Kirribilli House, an agreement you subsequently reneged on. Did you genuinely believe you'd cede the leadership to Keating sometime after the 1990 election or were you buying time?

'What?' Hawke snaps.

Were you genuine when you made the agreement?

In *Hawke: The Prime Minister* Blanche wrote, 'Hawke had called Keating's bluff and won. He had a leg-rope on his treasurer and his treasurer's supporters for two to three years.' It was this sentence that drove Keating into a revisionist frenzy.

In *Paul Keating: The Big-Picture Leader* he says, 'Blanche gave the game away in her book. She said Bob was very happy with the Kirribilli agreement. Why wouldn't he be?'

'Yeah ... ahhh ... but I've quoted what Paul said to me in my office.' (Keating told Hawke that if he didn't get a run at the PM's job, 'We'll be off to Europe. We won't be staying here – this is the arse-end of the world.') 'I don't want to go over it again because it's not very pleasant ...'

So you really were going to hand over the keys after the next election?

'Yeah, but until that time ...'

And you called Blanche that night ...

'Well, did I? Okay ...'

Was that because you had a sense that your time as prime minister was almost done and you'd soon have a new freedom?

'No, no, I just wanted to talk to her ...'

Keating also says that he, and not you, drove the Madrid Protocol that kept the miners out of Antarctica. He said that when he met with French prime minister Michel Rocard in 1988 they reached a deal to make Antarctica an 'environmentally protected zone'. He told Rocard he'd brief you when he got back to Australia. Did he?

'Not that I recall.' Hawke pauses. 'Look, it's recognised that Antarctica was me.'

Hawke laughs at the absurdity of having to explain something so obvious.

'One of the things about Paul is he did *so many things* for which he is responsible and did them so well and ... [laughs] ... he just had a tendency at times to claim a little bit more. But he didn't need to. Because he's one of the greatest members of parliament since Federation.'

A few months later, I'll contact Keating's office to arrange an interview. A phone call to his assistant Susan Grusovin meets with an unenthusiastic response. The return email the following week is even less pumped.

Keating, writes Grusovin, 'has no interest in any conversations about your book. He took note of your reference to Antarctica and his meeting with Prime Minister Michel Rocard in 1988. He said you might be interested in some of the press reporting of the period in respect of Antarctica, which may not come your way from Bob Hawke'.

The clippings from the *Sunday Telegraph* and the *Financial Review* are helpfully attached, with handwritten notes from Keating, in a PDF.

In one, from the *Financial Review*, 5 May 1989, with the headline HAWKE WAVERS ON ANTARCTIC TREATY, Ross Dunn reports: 'The Prime Minister, Mr Hawke, yesterday voiced his strong opposition to mining in Antarctica –' the next section is highlighted by Keating in yellow '– but refused to take a stand on the key issue which has deeply divided his Cabinet – whether to sign a new Antarctic Minerals Convention.'

In another highlighted passage from the story:

Mr Keating is wholly embracing environmental concerns in his efforts to prevent Australia signing an international minerals convention for Antarctica.

At his urging, Federal Cabinet will soon consider supporting Antarctica becoming a world park, or at the very least declaring Australia's territory a national park.

Mr Keating has proposed investigating the world park concept in his latest attempts to convince the Federal Government not to sign an international convention . . .

Hawke looks at me and pleads, 'Do we have to have much more of Paul?'

I tell Hawke that Bramston's book demands some kind of response.

'My point is,' says Hawke, 'I don't want to be seen as knocking Paul. I don't want to be seen as knocking Paul because I *genuinely* think he made a great contribution to Australia. *Outstanding.*'

What was the point of not retiring or ceding the leadership to Keating when it became apparent you didn't have the numbers? You called Col the night before and asked him to come up and stay with you. Did it seem absurd to you that the party would, for the first time in history, choose someone *less* popular?

'Well, I wasn't certain and I wasn't just going to lie down. I owed it to my supporters,' says Hawke.

The ballot was close, 56–51. If Hawke supporters Gareth Evans and Con Sciacca hadn't been out of town for the vote, two successful phone calls would've swayed it. Does Hawke ever reflect on the what-ifs?

'That's life,' he says. 'If your aunt had balls she'd be your uncle.'

Your pal Col says the next six weeks, as you transitioned from prime minister to unemployed sixty-two-year-old man, were pretty rough. Blanche describes you as being in a bad way psychologically.

'Awwww, I don't think I was in a bad way psychologically. In one sense, disappointed. But in another sense, I'd had a great life, you know. A very constructive one, done a lot, and it's not a fair assessment to say I was in a bad way psychologically. I knew there'd be good days ahead.'

Would it be accurate to say you feel a great affection, a love, for Keating?

'I . . . I . . . I . . . you know . . . I . . . [long pause] . . . *great respect*,' he says finally. 'Great respect.'

Sensing I've exhausted the issue, I move on.

I raise a topic that's been particularly controversial of late. Gay marriage. What are Hawke's views?

He throws his hands up to signal the stupidity of the question. 'Obviously in favour of it!' he says.

Now for the lighter part of the interview, I say.

Hawke brightens.

Death!

'Gah!'

How would you like your funeral to proceed, who will speak and in what order?

'Oh I haven't thought about that in any detail,' says Hawke. 'Plenty of time for it.'

What songs will be played?

'"Ode to Joy", the final movement of Beethoven's Ninth. I love that.'

Are you agnostic or an atheist?

'Ah . . . agnostic with a slight question mark.'

You've told Blanche that when death comes you'll be like your dad, that you won't be any trouble and that yours will be an easy death.

Hawke becomes exasperated.

'I just don't think about dying! I've never been worried by death and I'm not now. I just don't think about it! A lot of people do! *I don't!*'

Fair enough. Why should he rake over the bones of a working relationship that ended twenty-six years earlier or ponder the finer details of a state funeral, however fun that might be for the interviewer?

Hawke sits in perpetual warmth on the terrace of a house that hangs off one of the most divine positions on Sydney Harbour, a house oriented to steal the sun's every ray.

'A good place to smoke a cigar,' he says.

It is the winter of an important man's life. And although age gives no man an easy pass and Hawke carries all the accoutrements of ageing – the pacemaker, the uncooperative feet, a hearing aid, a beautifully ravaged face – he isn't one to complain.

He enjoys the deafness age has wrought upon him ('The quiet! I'm so happy!') and he has his daily, dementia-busting sudokus and cryptics to smash. He still commands media attention, China craves his business and political acumen, and every earthly want and whim has long been satisfied.

More, he has the woman he fell in love with forty years ago, and married twenty years later, in his bed every night.

And when your face is aimed at the autumn sun, there's a cigar in your paw and a crossword to finish, all those old squabbles do seem irrelevant.

'I couldn't be happier,' he says.

He looks down. Smiles at something. Lost in memories? More like fortified by a good life.

'You know the way out,' he says.

ACKNOWLEDGEMENTS

How unexpected life is. One minute I'm swinging an ambitious pitch at a cocktail party, the next the door to every significant figure in recent history is swung open.

To John Howard, who didn't walk out when I was forced to whisper the word 'cunt' in the context of a John Singleton quote, and to his assistants Sally Murphy and Ruth Gibson, thank you.

To Gareth Evans, for your candour and delightful sprinklings of Latin, as well as your lightning responses to emailed queries, thank you.

To Kim Beazley, who was as kind and as forthright as you'd expect of someone admired on both sides of politics, thank you.

To Dick Woolcott, for stories almost too good to be true, thank you.

To Col Cunningham, who eventually consented to an interview even though he was convinced it would be a doomed affair and who charmed me, like he's charmed everyone else over the past eighty-something years, thank you.

To Louis Pratt, who put down the levers of his 3D printer in the middle of a $300,000 commission for the interview, thank you.

To John Singleton, who is anything but a dull bulb, thank you.

To Ross Garnaut, who gave me two interviews in one day and who didn't show me the door when I mixed up monetary and fiscal policy, thank you.

To my parents, Cam and Kay, for your patience, kindness and counsel, thank you.

To my brother, Grant, whose writing I stole to win a prize in grade seven, thank you.

To Jeanne Ryckmans, the literary agent who delivered me this prize, thank you.

To Pan Macmillan's formidable team, Angus Fontaine, Rebecca Hamilton, Libby Turner, Daniel New and the book's editor Ali Lavau, thank you.

To Richard Freeman, for shooting a cover that stole my breath, thank you.

To Jill Saunders, for your diary keeping and wry humour, thank you.

To Blanche, the wife, the brilliant author, original thinker and peerless Sunday lunch companion, I thank you.

And to Bob Hawke, who consented to the book without meeting me and who patiently put down his sudokus and cryptic crosswords every Wednesday at three o'clock for an hour, sometimes two, of what might've seemed at the time as very odd lines of questioning, thank you. *Thank you.*

SELECTED ENDNOTES

11. 'His Majesty's Masturbators, as Eleanor...': d'Alpuget, *The Young Lion*, HarperCollins, 2013, p. 4.

19. 'I've been around in public...': National Press Club, Channel 10 News, 2 March 1983, https://www.youtube.com/watch?v=4DgabQbdiUk

20. 'Would you care to comment...': National Press Club, Channel 10 News, 2 March 1983, https://www.youtube.com/watch?v=4DgabQbdiUk

21. 'like some mythic figure...': McGregor, *Time of Testing*, Penguin Books, 1983, p. 22.

22. 'Leadership is not about being...': Keating, National Press Club, 1990, http://press-files.anu.edu.au/downloads/press/p291051/html/ch03.xhtml?referer=&page=10

22. 'Paul's performance was vainglorious and...': Hawke, *The Hawke Memoirs*, Heinemann Australia, 1994, p. 498.

22. 'Keating was a saboteur, pure...': Hawke, *The Hawke Memoirs*, Heinemann Australia, 1994, p. 536.

24. As one university don described...: d'Alpuget, *Robert J. Hawke*, Schwartz, 1982, p. 61.

24. 'It was in between overs...': Cricket Network, 'Handscomb on his ton, his dismissal - and Bob Hawke!', 4 January 2017, http://www.cricket.com.au/video/peter-handscomb-bob-hawke-australia-press-conference-pakistan-third-test-day-two-scg-highlights/2017-01-04)

25. In 1983, one economics writer...: McGregor, *Time of Testing*, Penguin Books, 1983, p. 29.

25. 'He physically couldn't stand, except...': d'Alpuget, *Robert J. Hawke*, Schwartz, 1982, pp. 97-8.

32. The 2010 telemovie *Hawke* opens . . . : Network Ten, *Hawke*, 2010.

38. 'It's just an unarguable case . . .': Koziol, *Sydney Morning Herald*, '"Absurd": Bob Hawke blasts lack of will to legalise euthanasia', 14 April 2016.

43. Does the brotherhood rhetoric match . . . : MacCallum, *The Good, the Bad and the Unlikely*, Black Inc, 2012, p. 145.

44. Gough Whitlam called Woolcott, 'Australia's . . .': Woolcott, Richard, *Undiplomatic Activities*, Scribe, 2007, p. 3.

54. 'When the rate of return . . .': Picketty, Thomas, *Capital in the Twenty-First Century*, 2013, p. 1.

55. 'By 1990 no Australian child . . .': Hawke, 23 June 1987, via http:// electionspeeches.moadoph.gov.au/speeches/1987-bob-hawke and https://melbourneinstitute.com/downloads/publications/ Poverty%20Lines/AER%201987.pdf

59. She describes your life at . . . : d'Alpuget, Blanche, *On Longing*, Melbourne University Press, 2008, p. 24.

60. 'He suggested a time, a . . .': d'Alpuget, Blanche, *On Longing*, Melbourne University Press, 2008, pp. 59–60.

62–3. Now, twenty years on, the show . . . : *60 Minutes*, Channel Nine, 29 January 2017.

63. 'When Hazel died in 2013 . . .': Murphy, 'Hazel: a rock star's rock, a nation's role model', *Sydney Morning Herald*, 25 May 2013.

64. Devine claimed Blanche stole Hazel's . . . : Devine, 'A Slap in the Face of History', *The Sunday Times*, 2 July 2011.

73. d'Alpuget, *Hawke: The Prime Minister*, Melbourne University Press, 2010, p. 137.

74–5. 'I will always remember my . . .': Hawke, 'Time to recognise the state of Palestine', *Australian Financial Review*, 13 February 2017.

75. 'Bibi will reply, 'What kind . . .': Henderson, 'Netanyahu shows failings of Hawke-Rudd call for Palestinian state', *The Australian*, 25 February 2017.

75. The Victorian Labor MP Michael . . . : Lewis, 'Labor 'heroes' accused of provoking Benjamin Netanyahu ahead of Australia visit', *The Australian*, 21 February 2017.

76. *The Australian*'s foreign affairs writer . . . : Sheridan, 'Labor's Hawke, Rudd and Evans invite ridicule by maligning Israel', *The Australian,* 25 February 2017.

77. In diplomatic cables published by . . . : 'Hawke would have quit over Israel', *Jewish News*, 12 April 2013.

82. 'In a sort of surrogate . . . ': Hawke, 'In The Family - The Beazleys', *Australian Story*, http://www.abc.net.au/austory/transcripts/s401435.htm.

86. And according to Beazley's biographer . . . : ibid.

88. In his final speech to . . . : Hawke, 19 December 1991, http://australianpolitics.com/1991/12/19/bob-hawke-final-speech-as-pm.html

93. It took eighteen months of . . . : 'The Madrid Protocol', *Australian Antarctic Division: Leading Australia's Antarctic Program*, Australian Government Department of Environment and Energy, http://www.antarctica.gov.au/law-and-treaty/the-madrid-protocol

96. 'I was devastated and overwhelmed . . . ': Hawke, *The Hawke Memoirs*, Heinemann Australia, 1994, pp. 192

97. 'If you kick him it . . . ': ibid, p. 196.

97. 'I was accused of being . . . ': ibid, p. 263.

103. Earlier in the year, the . . . : Robinson, 'Oxford's Cecil Rhodes statue must fall – it stands in the way of inclusivity', *The Guardian*, 19 January 2016, https://www.theguardian.com/commentisfree/2016/jan/19/rhodes-fall-oxford-university-inclusivity-black-students

126. Hawke's youngest daughter Rosslyn was . . . : d'Alpuget, *Robert J. Hawke*, Schwartz, 1982, p. 194.

127. Joh also told Police . . . : Metcalf, 'Sir Joh Bjelke-Petersen had secret deal with police ahead of 1971 Springbok tour protest', *Courier Mail*, 28 February 2013, http://www.couriermail.com.au/news/queensland/sir-joh-bjelke-petersen-had-secret-deal-with-police-ahead-of-1971-springbok-tour-protest/news-story/d0d8fe62bb09fa800463e895dfe4778f

127. 'The police took Joh at his . . . ': User 1735099, '1971 Springbok Tour', kevgillett.net, 1 March 2013, http://www.kevgillett.net/?p=7354

134. In 1990, the Investor Responsibility . . . : Wren, 'As Mandela Stumps for Sanctions, South Africa Debates Them', *New York Times*, 30 June 1990, http://www.nytimes.com/1990/06/30/world/as-mandela-stumps-for-sanctions-south-africa-debates-them.html

134–5. 'The whole process was self-reinforcing . . .': Evans, Nelson Mandela Day Address, Government House, Sydney, 17 July 2012, http://www.gevans.org/speeches/speech475.html

140. A secret CIA report from . . . : Stewart, 'CIA secret assessment: Bob Hawke brash, Gareth Evans brilliant', *The Australian*, 24 May 2016, http://www.theaustralian.com.au/national-affairs/foreign-affairs/cia-secret-assessment-bob-hawke-brash-gareth-evans-brilliant/news-story/c0a99ae52b51827c0d0515505db673ec

144. 'Hawke snarled back: 'I was . . . ': Evans, *Inside the Hawke Government: A Cabinet Diary*, Melbourne University Press.

165. I read aloud Beck's remarks . . . : Beck, as quoted in 'Beck Tries Out Decency', *The New Yorker*, 14 November 2016, http://www.newyorker.com/magazine/2016/11/14/glenn-beck-tries-out-decency

168. 'Nuclear power would be a . . . ': Kinninment, 'Bob Hawke pushes nuclear power at Woodford Folk Festival north of Brisbane', *ABC News*, 28 December 2016.

170. A viability analysis by the . . . : 'Nuclear Fuel Cycle Royal Commission Report', Government of South Australia, May 2016, https://yoursay.sa.gov.au/system/NFCRC_Final_Report_Web.pdf

185. In an article for *The Australian* . . . : Keating, 'Paul Keating: Libs are making it up', *The Australian*, 26 June 2007, http://www.theaustralian.com.au/opinion/paul-keating-libs-are-making-it-up/news-story/300a6a00685167e50e8442bccc0b3249?nk=8fe2f2166e25b28bba822c2084def0f3-1507450809

192. The right-wing columnist Andrew Bolt . . . : Bolt, 'The ultimate Labor party', *Herald Sun*, 11 December 2009.

192. 'I was certainly not offended . . . ': Staff reporter, 'Little Johnnie strips for Hawke's birthday bash', *Sydney Morning Herald*, 10 December 2009.

192. Hawke uses the occasion to . . . : AAP, 'Bob Hawke conferred honorary degree from Sydney University', *The Australian*, 9 December 2016.

193–6. 'It's a tremendous privilege to . . . ': Shorten quoted in AAP, 'Bob Hawke conferred honorary degree from Sydney University', *The Australian*, 9 December 2016.

199. Louis Pratt, the only child . . . : d'Alpuget, *On Longing*, Melbourne University Press, 2008, p. 17.

211. [He] was treated like a grandee . . . : d'Alpuget, *Robert J. Hawke*, Schwartz, 1982, p. 194.

214. 'Because I still have a . . . ': Hawke, 'The 1990-1991 Cabinet – transcript', National Archives of Australia, http://www.naa.gov.au/ collection/explore/cabinet/by-year/1990-1991/transcript-1990-91-cabinet.aspx

215. Richo responded by saying it . . . : 'Cabinet papers 1990-91: Richardson rejects Hawke ministry claims', *The Australian*, 1 January 2016.

219. 'Diplomatic cables from the Canadian . . .': Korski, 'Embassy Feared 1989 Chinese Raid Say Confidential Memos', 26 January 2015, https://www.blacklocks.ca/embassy-feared-1989-chinese-raid-say-confidential-memos/

220. Perceived by party leader Deng Xiaoping . . . : d'Alpuget, *Hawke The Prime Minister*, Melbourne University Press, 2010, p. 137.

221. In 2003, Monash University's director . . . : Banham, 'Children of the revolution', *Sydney Morning Herald,* 26 December 2003, http://www.smh.com.au/articles/2003/12/25/1072308628745.html

224. Four years later, Snedden would . . . : Robinson, 'Sir Billy and son "shared mystery lover"', *News.com*, http://www.news.com.au/ national/sir-billy-and-son-shared-mystery-lover/news-story/ 1c6084d46c09d0f13bb3ec96f0d06701)

225–7. He's popular among the Chinese . . . : d'Alpuget, *Hawke The Prime Minister*, Melbourne University Press, 2010, p. 124.

241. 'His polling shows that there . . . ': Hawke, 25 August 1988, https:// www.politicsforum.org/forum/viewtopic.php?t=34568

243. Tell me about the report . . . : Garnaut, 'Australia and the Northeast Asian Ascendancy', 1989.

252. In 1961, aged seventeen, Blanche . . . : d'Alpuget, 'Lust', taken from *Eleven Deadly Sins* by Ross Fitzgerald, Heinemann Australia, 1993.

253. 'I had had many lovers . . . : d'Alpuget, *On Longing*, Melbourne University Press, 2008, p. 15.

254. The pair met in Melbourne . . . : ibid, p. 21.

274. As one fellow student recalled . . . : d'Alpuget, *Robert J. Hawke*, Schwartz, 1982, p. 38.

283. According to Keating now . . . : Bramston, *Paul Keating: The Big Picture Leader*, Scribe Publishing, 2016, pp 309–10.

286. In one, from the *Financial Review* . . . : Dunn, 'Hawke wavers on Antarctic treaty', *Australian Financial Review*, 5 May 1989.

Grateful acknowledgement is given to Bob Hawke for permission to reproduce material from *The Hawke Memoirs* (Heinemann, 1994), as well as speeches, articles and interviews.

Grateful acknowledgement is also given to Blanche d'Alpuget for permission to reproduce material from *Robert J. Hawke* (Schwartz, 1982), 'Lust' from *Eleven Deadly Sins* (Heinemann, 1993), *On Longing* (MUP, 2008), *Hawke: The Prime Minister* (MUP, 2010) and *The Young Lion* (HarperCollins, 2013).

Extracts from *On Longing* and *Hawke: The Prime Minister* by Blanche d'Alpuget reproduced with permission of Melbourne University Publishing.

Extracts from *Robert J. Hawke* by Blanche d'Alpuget reproduced with permission of Schwartz and Black Inc Books.

Grateful acknowledgement is given to the Honourable Paul Keating for permission to reproduce the extract on page 35 from 'Paul Keating: The Libs are making it up', published in *The Australian*.

Extract on page 54 taken from *Capital in the Twenty-First Century* by Thomas Piketty, translated by Arthur Goldhammer, Cambridge, Mass.: The Belknap Press of Harvard University Press, Copyright © 2014 by the President and Fellows of Harvard College.

Grateful acknowledgement is given to Professor the Hon Gareth Evans AC for permission to reproduce his Nelson Mandela Day Address on pages 134–135.

Grateful acknowledgement is given to the Honourable Bill Shorten MP for permission to reproduce the speech on pages 193–196.

Extract on pages 214–215 from the 1990-1991 Cabinet transcript, reproduced by permission of the National Archives of Australia.

Extract on page 221 taken from 'Children of the revolution' published by the *Sydney Morning Herald,* reproduced by permission of Cynthia Banham and Fairfax Media Limited.

Extract on page 283 from *Paul Keating: The Big Picture Leader* by Troy Bramston reproduced by permission of the author and Scribe Publications.